George A. Maloney SJ

MYSTICISM
and the
NEW AGE

CHRISTIC CONSCIOUSNESS
IN THE NEW CREATION

ALBA · HOUSE   NEW · YORK

SOCIETY OF ST. PAUL, 2187 VICTORY BLVD., STATEN ISLAND, NEW YORK 10314

Library of Congress Cataloging-in-Publication Data

Maloney, George A., 1924 -
   Mysticism and the New Age : christic consciousness in the
new creation / by George Maloney.
       p.   cm.
   Includes bibliographical references.
   ISBN 0-8189-0596-4
   1. Mysticism. 2. Logos. 3. Spiritual life — Catholic authors.
   4. New Age movement.   I. Title.
   BV5082.2.M35 1990   90-44206
   248.22 — dc20   CIP

Imprimi Potest:
Rev. Bert Thelen, S.J.
Provincial of Wisconsin Province
of the Society of Jesus.

Designed, printed and bound in the United States of
America by the Fathers and Brothers of the
Society of St. Paul, 2187 Victory Boulevard,
Staten Island, New York 10314, as part of their
communications apostolate.

PRINTING INFORMATION:

Current Printing - first digit 1 2 3 4 5 6 7 8 9 10 11 12

Year of Current Printing - first year shown
  1991   1992   1993   1994   1995   1996   1997   1998

DEDICATION

To
Loretta Kelleher and Sylvia Hall Lockworth,
who have been
''new-agers'' in Christ,
even before
the term became popular.

ACKNOWLEDGMENTS

Sincere thanks to Suzy Caruther for having typed my manuscript, and for proofreading and for helpful suggestions from June Culver and Sister Joseph Agnes, S.C.H. I am indebted to Loretta Kelleher and Sylvia Hall Lockworth, who first suggested that I poll the opinions of about 150 leading "new agers" by a questionnaire and who helped in searching out for me addresses and vital articles and documents in my research for this book.

Deepest gratitude to the 65% of those polled in my questionnaire who so generously responded and shared with me their valuable insights.

Thanks are due to the Bruce Publishing Company for permission to use its translation of the New Testament as the basic text for N.T. citations: *The New Testament*, Part One: *The Four Gospels*, tr. by James A Kleist, S.J. and Part Two: *Acts of the Apostles, Epistles and Apocalypse*, tr. by Joseph L. Lilly, C.M. (Milwaukee, WI: The Bruce Publishing Company, 1956). Also to Darton, Longman & Todd, Ltd., and Doubleday & Co., Inc. for selected citations from *The Jerusalem Bible* (1966).

CONTENTS

Chapter Three: *A Logos Mysticism*

Chapter Six: A New Psychological Age

INTRODUCTION

The central aim of this book is to develop a spirituality, not entirely unknown in the Bible in the Church during her first thousand years, that will restore for us the sense of the numinous, of the sacred immanence of the divine in all of God's creations, including ourselves in our vital relationships with our planet and the entire universe.

We will explore Christianity to draw together elements from its ancient traditions to reinterpret a Logos mysticism, based on God's creation with human cooperation of all things in His Word. We will discover creation as a dynamic process revolving around the immanent, creative Logos in us human beings, made to find our uniqueness and freedom by contemplating the immanent Logos in all things. Synergistically we are called by God to work with the Logos, who is God in matter, Jesus Christ.

I pray that, as you read this book, you may experience what St. Paul described out of his own experiences: "If, then, anyone is in Christ, he is a new creation; the old state of things has gone; wonderful to tell, it has been made over, absolutely new! All this comes from the action of God, who has reconciled us to himself through Christ, and has entrusted us with this ministry of reconciliation. . . . We are, therefore, Christ's ambassadors. . . ." (2 Cor 5:17-20).

George A. Maloney, S.J.

St. Patrick's Novitiate
Midway City, CA
October 29, 1989

Mysticism and the New Age

1

The Beginning Of A New Age

A vast similitude interlocks all,
All spheres, grown, ungrown, small,
    large, suns, moons, planets,
All distances of place however wide,
All distances of time, all inanimate forms,
All souls, all living bodies though
    they be ever so different, or in
    different worlds,
All gaseous, watery, vegetable,
    mineral processes, the fishes, the brutes,
All nations, colors, barbarisms,
    civilizations, languages,
All identities that have existed or
    may exist on this globe or any globe,
All lives, and deaths, all of the
    past, present, future,
This vast similitude spans them, and
    always have spann'd,
And shall forever span them and
    completely hold and enclose them.

Walt Whitman

Would you deny that the human race has entered into a new age? We presently are too close to its launching to see where it will eventually lead us. We are like a teenager who gropes for meaningfulness in the new-founded powers that slowly emerge from within him.

As we enter into a new millennium with the 21st century we are tensioned between a feeling of pessimism, even fear, and an optimism that excites us with fanciful dreams of a world of infinite richness. Our new age is symbolized by our entrance into space exploration. We have walked with Neil Armstrong on the moon. Through satellite communication we are in immediate touch, not only with planet Earth and its people, but also with other planets as well. Our universe is shrinking in the sense that all parts of it are becoming more and more "present" to us. Infinity seems to be in our grasp!

FEAR OF THE NEW WORLD

Yet in another way, we stand in a frightened isolation "against" that unknown world, exploding before us into mysteries that we cannot handle with our limited, human knowledge. Dr. Harold Urey, one of the inventors of the atom bomb, wrote shortly after one of the early atomic explosions on the desert flats of New Mexico: "I am trying to frighten you. I am myself a frightened man. All the experts I know are also frightened."

It is reported that these experts waited for this explosion with faces to the ground. Even the most unbelieving of them felt something like a prayer rising in their hearts. It was like the prayer of a young squire on the eve of his being knighted. At that historic moment the human race ended its adolescence. We have entered into our new role of master of the uncreated!

As we learn how to split the atom and release powers that can rival the energies of the sun, we stand quivering with fright. What a power has been placed into our hands to transform the world! Or to destroy it! We cringe in our corner of this universe, afraid, feeling the need of a *Someone* beyond us. Someone ever more powerful than we are. Someone who, unlike us, is totally and consistently unselfish. Someone who is Love itself.

One way of coping with such multiple richness, power and apparent meaninglessness is to retreat into ourselves. We can build physical and psychological walls around us and try to live in "splendid isolation" from the rest of the world.

A NEW REVOLUTION

Another response to an exciting exploding world of immense power and richness is to join in the new revolution that is quietly taking place, especially in our Western world.

This is an upheaval of the habitual ways we consider ourselves, the world, God, science, politics and economics. It is a revolution that challenges our basic assumptions about who we are, what kind of a world we are living in and would like to live in during the coming ages.

In the words of Lewis Mumford, "Every transformation of man . . . has rested on a new metaphysical and ideological base; or rather, upon deeper stirrings and intuitions whose rationalized expression takes the form of a new picture of the cosmos and the nature of man."[1]

In *The Aquarian Conspiracy* Marilyn Ferguson describes a benign "conspiracy" that is rapidly triggering a new thinking. It is a "new mind" that gathers into its nebulous framework human potential psychologies, nuclear physics and Far Eastern religions as well as healing and channeling to receive new power through esoteric revelations from the "other side."[2]

Time magazine described this New Age movement as "a combination of spirituality and superstition, fad and farce, about which the only certain thing is that it is not new. . . . The underlying faith is a lack of faith in the orthodoxies of rationalism, high technology, routine living, spiritual law and order. Somehow, the New Agers believe, there must be some secret and mysterious shortcut or alternative path to happiness and health. And nobody dies."[3]

NEW PARADIGMS OF GLOBAL CHANGE

The aim of this chapter is to highlight the positive elements of this new thinking so that we can lay the foundations for a powerful inbreaking of God's Holy Spirit to bring about a Christian new age consciousness. The seeds of such a holistic, planetary thinking have been planted within the revelation of Jesus Christ. They have been unfolding as a faith consciousness received and developed in the social and cultural contexts of Christians down through the centuries.

Many of the valuable and seemingly revolutionary insights coming from such modern "new thinking" all too often had been lost in Christianity, especially in its Western form of scholastic theology, in its "masculine" legalism and organizational power. Other insights could only now be drawn forth as God reveals Himself more explicitly through modern nuclear physics, astronomy, global economics and geopolitics. Only a highly industrialized Western world with its consumerism could negatively call us into a love of nature and a vigilance to create a new harmony and balance in the ecological systems of our world.

I am, therefore, not concerned with presenting every aspect of the so-called new age thinking. Channeling, healing with crystals, the occult and witchcraft, reincarnation and what Shirley MacLaine teaches may be interesting topics. I am not interested in presenting these elements or analyzing specific practices in the light of traditional Christian teachings. Many books (mostly by

Evangelical fundamentalist Christians) have negatively criticized the New Age movement.[4]

I wish to present the outline of a new thinking that we see developing in the last three decades of the 20th century, especially in our Western industrialized world. Much of this thinking we Christians can and should accept, insofar as it is compatible with the basic truths of Christian revelation.

SHIFTS TO NEW PARADIGMS

In order that we may better understand the great shifts in global consciousness that has been quietly evolving within the minds and hearts of about five to ten percent of reflective persons in our Western world, let us turn for a moment to Thomas Kuhn's concept of paradigm shifts.

Kuhn, a science historian and philosopher, in his important book *The Structure of Scientific Revolutions*,[5] helps us to understand changes in belief systems that provide us with new breakthroughs and insights. These allow first individuals, then whole cultures, to become liberated from the limits imposed by an earlier model of reality to embrace a new and better model.

For Kuhn, a *paradigm* (in Greek, this means a *pattern*) is a scheme for understanding and explaining certain aspects of reality. Shifts in paradigms have resulted in greater understanding of reality in the fields of education, medicine, theology, philosophy, sociology, economics, etc. A new paradigm is a distinctly new way of thinking about old problems, but with fresh insights and greater penetration into a wholeness in multiplicity.

THE COPERNICAN REVOLUTION

A clear example of such a paradigm shift was the way that Nicolaus Copernicus blew apart Ptolemy's system that posited the

Earth as the center of the universe. Copernicus proved scientifi-
cally that the Earth moves around the sun once a year and daily
rotates on its axis.

Galileo and Kepler developed Copernicus' insights, but the
ideas of Copernicus had already started a new paradigm that tallied
better with reality than the model from the Middle Ages. He
destroyed Aristotle's idea of a fixed Earth and the medieval concept of a man-centered world, and proved that the Earth is not the
center of the universe.

Copernicus launched a new consciousness revolution by making empirical, scientific knowledge the determinant of what was
true and real. No longer was religious tradition the sole carrier of
truth. Now it was the scientist who observed an objective world that
opened up its secrets to those who strictly followed the new
methodology of science.

A CARTESIAN WORLD

In order that we may see the radical shift in consciousness that
is now taking place, we need to understand what our shift had come
out of. It was Rene Descartes in the 17th century who believed that
the key to understanding the universe lay in discovering its logical
order. He invented new mathematical forms to express this logic of
nature. All of nature, he thought, was "static" and obedient to
basic, universal laws. Descartes is perhaps most responsible for the
split in the way we conceive ourselves as human beings. He saw us
as having two parts: mind and body. We were for him a "res
cogitans," a thinking thing, but also a "res extensa," a material
body. Yet his famous dictum put the emphasis upon the importance
of the mind over the body. "Ego cogito; ergo sum": "I think;
therefore, I am." We human beings are minds, caught inside a
material body that eventually will die, while we will live forever
because of our immortal soul.

Such a split within the human person was projected outward. All around us exists a multitude of separated objects. It is our mind that looks at this unchangeable world and discovers its universal laws. Isaac Newton built his mechanistic world view upon this separation of mind and matter. Newtonian physics prevailed until the 20th century, when the age of nuclear physics brought about a new shift in understanding God, the individual human person, the Earth and the entire cosmos.

Most of us have grown up with a Newtonian understanding of the universe, of God and of ourselves. In this paradigm God was "up there," a static observer of a mechanical world. He directed the world though the laws of mechanics He built into the cosmos. It was constructed on the three-dimensional space of Euclidean geometry. "Out there" existed as an absolute space, an "empty container," in which all physical phenomena occurred.

All changes were described in terms of another absolute called *time*. Like space, it had no connection with material objects. It flowed independently from the past through the present to the future. What moved through absolute space and time were material particles called atoms: small, solid and indestructible things, the basic building blocks for all material creatures.

AN ENERGIZED COSMOS OF
INTER-RELATIONSHIPS

In 1905 Albert Eisntein published his special theory of relativity and "slew a beautiful theory with an ugly fact," in the words of T.H. Huxley. Einstein proved that Newton's absolute space can no longer be considered as an independent absolute. Both space and time are interrelated and form a fourth-dimensional continuum which physicists today, using Einstein's term, call "space-time," to show that all reality is relational.

Einstein showed that mass in any material object has nothing to do with a solid, independent substance, but is rather a form of energy. Now energy and mass are interchangeable. $E=Mc^2$ means that the energy of a given event is measured by the mass times the ''constant'' squared. For Einstein the invariable in every relative observation is the speed of light, 186,000 miles per second.

Therefore, the human person is not a detached observer but a participator. Energy rearranges itself in new forms by creating new relationships with the surrounding environment in which it is released. The constant, regardless of space and time or the position and velocity of the observer, will always be measured by the speed of light.

Now the concepts of space and time are only elements of a language used by an observer to describe an environment in which he/she is a vital part. No scientist can be ''detached'' from the environment being observed. Such a person is a part of the whole. Language is used to describe a part of reality, but never can be the full reality. The scientist is both actor and spectator — in a word, an active participator in changing relationships between him/herself and what is being measured or observed. Now we conceive the universe as a participatory place of dynamic, energizing inter-relationships.

Norman Pittinger, a process theologian, well describes such a dynamic universe:

> *We live in and we are confronted by a richly inter-connected, inter-related, inter-penetrative series of events, just as we ourselves are such a series of events.* [6]

In such a view, all of us are a part of God's entire creation. We are more than a microcosm of the macrocosm. We are a *hologram* — that is, a part of an image that, when illumined by a laser beam, seems suspended in three-dimensional space and as a piece contains the entire image. We are the consciousness, the love-spark that can ignite the whole and lead the entire universe with God's graceful power into a unity of diversity.

Our very bodies are made up of the same matter that makes up the stars. We find the same calcium in our bodies which is found in the sea. But we have the unique power to ''en-spirit'' the matter of the universe, not only into ourselves, but into a unity of one body through love. We enter into the world of mystery and inter-relatedness. Everything is dynamically in movement, in intimate relationships.

God is seen now as energizing Love, bombarding all of His creation from inside as well as from outside. He should no longer be conceived by us as a God up there or over there, but as a personalized energy of love interacting with all His creatures, ordering all seeming chaos into higher levels of loving unity. He leads the universal dance of all things in harmonious, yet in-dividualized motion, stretching toward greater complexity and yet greater union in multiplicity. This God is truly, as St. Paul preached to the Athenians, not far from us, ''For in him we live and move and have our being'' (Ac 17:28).

THREE DIFFERENT VIEWS OF REALITY

How can we stand outside of this dynamic universe of which we are such a vital, energized part, and comprehend something of this new consciousness-development going on in our contempor-ary world? I have been helped greatly by Dr. Willis Harman, emeritus professor of engineering-economic systems at Stanford University and present president of the Institute of Noetic Sciences in Sausalito, CA. If we borrow from his scheme of systems-changes that he insists are evident in our present world, we may bring to the consciousness movement some sort of schematic overview and more clearly understand the momentous happening in our world-consciousness today.

See pg 54 N.A. Almanac

We have already described what the scientific revolution, especially in the 17th and 18th centuries, brought to society's basic belief of reality. In such a system scientific knowledge was the only true and valid knowledge available to us moderns. Any knowledge derived through religious faith was considered atavistic and "unenlightened."

Quantified matter is seen as the supreme reality. Any mental processes fall under true reality insofar as they can be measured by brain changes. The objective order is superior to any subjective experiences. The latter, since they cannot be rigorously tested and observed by the scientific method, partake of a minor value at best. There can be no ultimate goal or purpose to the created universe and no divine Creator since neither of these can be tested by science. Ultimately, if science is supreme and the only true source of knowledge, then there can be no human consciousness that survives the death of the brain.

In order to show a profound change that is shaking the premises of Newtonian physics, Harman outlines three varying views of reality by which persons today line-up their belief systems. In a word, he sketches three differing *metaphysics*:

> M-1: *Materialistic Monism*
> (Matter giving rise to mind)
> M-2: *Dualism*
> (Matter plus mind)
> M-3: *Transcendental Monism*
> (Mind giving rise to matter)

M-1 exalts science as positivistic and reductionistic. True reality is always quantified. Such scientific knowledge has to be the only true knowledge we can have and that there is. Human consciousness in view of reality is only a part of the material brain and cannot be studied or known beyond observing the physical brain.

M-2 posits a dualistic source of true knowledge. Matter-energy stuff is the object of scientific study. Mind-spirit is another component of created reality and can yield true knowledge by exploring it with other methods than positivistic science. This knowledge has been developed by various psychologies to study the world of individual inner consciousness and even the unconscious.

M-3 makes the gigantic leap from both M-1 and M-2 to develop a metaphysics whose ultimate stuff of the universe is *consciousness*. Here is where Dr. Harman boldly maintains that a major transformation is taking place at the most fundamental level of the belief structure of Western industrial society. Such a change signals a view of reality as profound as the scientific revolution that four centuries ago forever altered the way we view the world.

THE WORLD COMES FROM CONSCIOUSNESS

Harman confesses that to maintain such a belief, namely, that consciousness gave rise to matter, sounds incredible, even to the present majority of Westerners. The M-3 view of reality is not anything new in human history. For thousands of years it has been the basis of true reality in most of the world's spiritual traditions. This inner enlightenment or *gnosis* — that is, an awakening from out of sleepy darkness to live in the light of new awareness in unity with God and the entire universe — has been called in human history the *perennial wisdom*. The mystical writings of most spiritual traditions, Christian, Jewish, Sufi, Hindu or Buddhist, all give testimony to such an inner understanding of reality similar to M-3.

Dr. Harman gives an explanation of M-3:

In our ordinary state the world seems real; various kinds of events take place, and there are apparent causal relationships among them. Some of these relationships are so dependable, in fact, that we discover "scientific laws" to describe them. (Only rarely does mind seem to intrude in the physical world in such a way that anomalous phenomena occur.) But suppose one "awakens" from the "dreams" of the physical world. It then becomes apparent that the causality law is different than we thought (and were taught): "I, the dreamer" (or "We, the collective dreamer") am the cause of the events and the relationships. The out-of-consciousness collective=universal mind is creator of the world which the conscious individual mind experiences. [8]

He cautions that in presenting these different metaphysics, he is not arguing that only M-3 is the true way of looking at reality in our modern society. What he intends by highlighting M-3 as the belief system for today is to show that it is ''more congenial'' to the totality of human experience than is M-1 with its positivistic, reductionistic scientific worldview. [9]

NUCLEAR PHYSICS AND GOD

We need not be nuclear physicists or astronomers to accept the changing view of our universe as given to us by these people. And how revolutionary and different is our modern view of the world as compared to that of Copernicus' or Newton's world! Let us look at this exciting view of a universe in flux moving through a conscious field of energy from seeming chaos to some ordered unity in multiplicity.

Physicists around the world in specially constructed cyclotrons uncovered new particles in the subatomic world. Relentlessly they sought to find the ultimate basic unit of matter, that from which all reality has its being. Einstein, until his dying days, resisted the thinking of some physicists that randomness could be the ultimate reality.

And yet as these scientists probed deeper, they came closer to harmonizing the findings of Einstein's theory of relativity with their ''quanta'' chaos and seeming disorder as they moved away from an exclusive M-1 to embrace more and more an M-3 view of reality.

Murray Gel-Mann in 1963 discovered that the more than 200 subatomic particles were made up of three smaller building blocks. These he called *quarks*. But these could not be defined by any relative position or peculiar pattern of activity. They were distinguished by their properties, especially the degree of electric charge they carried. Now the theory of relativity shines through the language used by quantum physicists to describe the qualities of these quarks. As human consciousness can never be separated from the material world around it, the language of human qualities and inter-relationships becomes the language of physicists in the nuclear age.

The human observer is involved in subatomic particles and their activities. Contrasts and similarities produce ''human'' terms for the more recently discovered five quarks as the basic units of all matter: ''up,'' ''down,'' ''strange,'' ''charm,'' and ''beauty.'' As quarks come in pairs, physicists believe there should be a sixth quark, which will pair up with ''beauty'' and will be called ''truth.''

This highlights Einstein's theory of relativity and suggests through such human qualities given to quarks that the ''perceptual unit'' of us human beings and ''it'' are parts of the basic structure of all matter. Human consciousness is involved in the creation of the world, and the material world helps to form human consciousness. Yet behind it all, Einstein insisted, was a Supreme Orderer. We are dealing with fields of force and energy and no longer with independent, solid entities. All creatures are being moved by a Super-Consciousness that creates matter through inter-relationships. Molecules, whose electrons generate a force in one area, like a magnet, affect us, the ''outsiders,'' who really can never be outside of the material world around us. Nor can God in His infinite, uncreated energies of love!

NETWORKS OF INTER-RELATIONSHIPS

We see now that the material world around us and within the microcosm of our bodies exists — or better — is being created and is evolving through complex events of energy inter-relationships. Fritjof Capra well describes what the quantum theory leads us to as a new vision of the universe and of our inter-relationships with each part of the whole:

> *Quantum theory forces us to see the universe not as a collection of physical objects, but rather as a complicated web of relations between the various parts of a unified whole. This, however, is the way in which Eastern mystics have experienced the world, and some of them have expressed their experience in words which are almost identical with those used by atomic physicists.* [10]

In all religions that have maintained a mystical view of the immanence of a personalized divinity inside of all created things, the goal of human wisdom is to experience the unity of all diverse creatures in the Absolute One. A world of separated objects is considered in such mystical traditions as an illusion created by man's rational powers. Inner discipline, especially through transcendental meditation of the ''insideness'' of the Divine One, leads us out of what Hinduism calls ''maya'' or a state of living in darkness, illusion, dreaming and unreality.

Today many quantum physicists speak in M-3 perspectives of inter-relationships of all things to each other, and the unity of all in a wholeness, that resembles the language of mystics. Einstein wrote the following statement because he had experienced through his experiments and personal insights that religion without science is impossible and science without religion is incomplete:

The most beautiful and most profound emotion we can experience is the sensation of the mystical. It is the sower of all true science. He to whom this emotion is a stranger, who can no longer wonder and stand rapt in awe, is as good as dead. To know that what is impenetrable to us really exists, manifesting itself as the highest wisdom and the most radiant beauty which our dull faculties can comprehend only in their most primitive forms — this knowledge, this feeling is at the center of true religiousness. [11]

NON-DUALITY

For the Western mind good is opposed to bad, birth to death, the finite to the infinite. But to oppose God as infinite to everything else as finite is to set up a false duality. God's plenitude cannot be placed within an oppositional duality. The Hindu *Advaita* or non-duality is a theological statement that flows out of an in-depth experience of God as the ocean of being in which a human being floats as a drop of the whole. It preserves the mystery that cannot be unraveled through an intellectual process as in M-1 metaphysics, but which can be approached only in the darkness of paradoxes.

The Hindu Upanishads express this mystery:

He is not known by him who knows Him, not understood by him who understands. He alone contemplates Him who has ceased to contemplate Him. In all knowledge as thought by intuition, the wise man finds Him. It is in Him alone, the Atman, *that each one is strong. It is in knowing Him alone that one becomes immortal. A great loss it is, in truth, for him who does not attain Him here below.*

For the Far Eastern or Eastern Christian contemplative, to explain the union of God and ourselves and the material world by any limiting concepts is to mock the real experience. And yet, any contemplative, from either East or West, knows from experience, once he/she has entered into the interior castle, that God is never an object to be looked at and petitioned, to be controlled by one's intellect in cold objectivity. God is experienced as present to the contemplative as breath is in the breather.

ENLIGHTENMENT

We cannot live in relationship to our material world, to God, to ourselves and to other human beings exclusively according to the classical framework that evolved in the Western world through Aristotle and Newton. Such a vision denies holism, the sense of the unity of all beings and the mutual belonging to each other through dependent interacting relationships.

This had been the teaching of all religions that have maintained the non-classical, mystical tradition. Enlightenment or *samadhi* comes when one breaks through the binding grip of the filter system of human discursive thought that prevents one from entering into the dynamic environment of energies and material creatures to come to experience the oneness of all things in the Absolute One:

> *Entering into the samadhi of purity, (one obtains) all penetrating insight that enables one to become conscious of the absolute oneness of the universe.* [12]

A CALL TO AN INNER JOURNEY

The whole area of mind, of expanded consciousness, of the inner, spiritual world, is drawing a small but ever-growing segment of people who are eager and willing to embrace a new global consciousness of their oneness with all of created nature, with all human beings as brothers and sisters of the one human family, with God as the Source of all our happiness and ultimate meaningfulness. Like the Israelites in the Sinai Desert, these modern pilgrims into the deserts of their hearts are willing to move farther away from the enslavement in which the exclusive Newtonian scientific model has been pontificating for 300 years what is true and what is false. They move out for the Promised Land that can be reached only through the inward journey into greater global consciousness.

Such people have seen how modern technology, the mas--culine "animus" culture, has created its own Frankenstein monster. The earth's deposit of natural resources is rapidly being consumed, leaving slag heaps in oceans of garbage. Fumes from machines rise up to cloud the atmosphere with a gaseous curtain that may eventually throttle any green life on planet Earth.

Such gigantic problems that face our modern society can never be solved primarily by more technology or more education, but by a better knowledge of our relationships to earth, to other human beings, to ourselves and to God. It is a question of becoming rooted in God, by embracing a *theocentric* vision of the universe where a loving, all-powerful, now-creating God is the Center of all reality.

We need to create and live by a new system of ethical values that go beyond one's own self-interests. What is needed is a new theological anthropology of human beings as cosmic citizens, not merely of America or of planet Earth, but of the entire universe. We are all inter-related and what we do to the universe, we eventually do to ourselves.

Such a planetary consciousness will make nations and individuals realize their collective responsibility for discovering and sharing knowledge about natural systems and how they are affected by human activities and vice versa. But the greatest need and greatest urgency for a change of values is that we change our interior vision. Saving mankind from isolation and alienation will not be done by mere negative motivation, through fear of a final cataclysmic war if we do not dispel the pollution of our inner spirits.

A PERSONALIZED LOVING CENTER

This can come only in a newness of religious insight that all human beings and all of our material cosmos are inter-related and inter-dependent, through a sense of community, of belonging and sharing together the riches that God has so abundantly given to all His creatures. It is through interior prayer, living contact with God as a personalized loving Center in humble loving adoration that we will be able to touch God as the Circle that has no circumference, and yet embraces each of His creatures in the unity of His dynamic loving creativity.

It is only in such intimate oneness with God as our Center that we can receive living knowledge that is the same as transforming love. Only such experienced love will allow us to see our unique place in the whole of creation that forms one unity in God. Transformed by such oneness with the Center we can stretch out, one in the same creative power of God, creatively to work to bring about a better universe.

Let us turn to this Divine Center of all reality and see how God meant ourselves and all other creatures to grow into greater and greater harmony and oneness through creative work to build the universe and no longer destroy it and ourselves in the same process.

2

Developing An Earth Spirituality

As we enter into the 21st century, one of the most urgently needed areas of reflection and growth in human awareness is that of developing an Earth spirituality. We are guided in our cultural codings by myths or stories that help us to grasp the mystery of reality which daily faces us.

God's creative Spirit is sending forth a universal call for us to let go and die to the outmoded myths or stories that have been guiding our thinking and our actions since the industrial revolution gave us the illusion that we are the masters of our universe.

Authors speak of various kinds of story-telling as a reflection of our human conciousness attempting to describe a given part of reality. In the words of Joan Didion:

> *We tell ourselves stories in order to live. We look for the sermon in the suicide, for the social or moral lesson in the murder of five. We interpret what we see, select the most workable of the multiple choices. We live entirely . . . by the imposition of a narrative line upon disparate images, by the "ideas" with which we have learned to freeze the shifting phantasmagoria which is our actual experience.* [1]

Many people today are asking with greater penetration and urgency just who they are. The answers given to them by Newtonian physics and Western Christianity, that so radically separated human beings from God and from the material nature around them, will no longer give adequate directions to solve the cataclysmic problems that are blanketing our world.

The consciousness, self-realization and human potential movements seemingly only foster more anthropocentrism, all too often adding to the problems. We need a myth or story which, when told today, best gets to the core of our human drama and can help us to ultimate meaningfulness both for our human lives, and for the entire universe of which we are so vitally and intrinsically united. We need a "plot-line," as novelists speak of. We are searching for a coherent narrative line around which we can weave a new story that best presents us with meaningfulness in the chaotic world of the 21st century.

A SPIRITUALITY
OF THE SACREDNESS OF MATTER

We desperately need a spirituality that will restore for us the sense of the sacred immanence of the divine in all of God's creation, including ourselves in our vital relationships with our world.

The heavily rationalistic spirituality which has served to present Christianity to the West, is in need of a complementary vision. Such a "new" vision was actually found in stone-age societies and continues even today in the spirituality of the North American Indians.

It is grounded more in perceptual, intuitive knowledge. It is an openness to God as mystery whom we meet in a reverential awe and wonderment as transcendent and also immanently dwelling within all of His material creation. As Jesus Christ is the meeting of divinity and humanity, with neither of them inseparable and yet each of them a distinct nature, so also we and the whole of creation in all of our materiality and finiteness are not to be separated from God living with us and all of nature.

This chapter focuses upon the urgency of building a holistic spirituality by creating a global consciousness of our oneness with God's Spirit and with all living and non-living systems throughout the universe. We are desperately in need of a spiritual corrective that will offset the imbalance that comes by placing ourselves as the center of the universe. Such a vision has made us dominators, exploiters and even exterminators of nature which we see as our enemy to be conquered and used for our own unenlightened purposes.

We have lost God and the Source and Goal of all His creation and have made ourselves the center of all reality. This brings a slow psychic and spiritual death through the suffocating blanket of meaninglessness that covers our earthly existence.[2] It is not that we are ignorant of the impending doom that could face our planet. But most of us lack the inner directing force to unleash unknown psychic and creative spiritual powers to transform such problems into opportunities of creating a new age of oneness among all God's creatures in peace and justice.

About a decade ago, Patricia Mische interviewed hundreds of children in grade and high schools. Over 80% believed that a nuclear war was inevitable before the year 2000. Most believed worldwide hunger, pollution, unemployment, inflation and economic problems will be worse. They felt powerless before the complexity and global scale of these problems. They felt there are no solutions and questioned whether there is going to be a future. And in light of that ultimate doubt about species survival, they questioned whether their personal lives had any meaning.[3]

MEANINGLESSNESS TO HUMAN EXISTENCE

Adults even more have an abiding pessimism about the future of the world and are plagued by a sense of futility to their lives. The Austrian psychiatrist, Viktor E. Frankl, explained: "Effectively an ever-increasing number of our clients today suffer from a feeling of interior emptiness — which I have described as existential emptiness — a feeling of total absence of a meaning to existence."[4]

Dr. Frankl attributes this present existential emptiness to the forfeiture of instinct and the loss of tradition. Man's instinct does not tell him, as animals' instinct does, what he *must* do. Because he has cut himself off from the roots of his past by throwing away traditions, he is at a loss as to what he *ought* to do. Usually he finds himself in the position that he does not know what he *wants* exactly. The result of this is conformism in the West and totalitarianism in the East.[5]

NEGATIVE CAUSES FOR LACK OF HARMONY

We have lost our intimacy with an immanent, active, loving divine community living within us and in all creatures. We do not know how beautiful we are and how creatively we can build our world into a loving community because we have lost God as the sacred, holy and all beautiful community of Love, who draws each of His children made according to His very own image and likeness into a participation in His holiness.

Newtonian physics gave us a God who was static, perfect and immutable. Descartes defined the human person as a thinking being, observing with no living relationship a reified universe. A human being was a thinking soul, separable from matter and the whole material world through thought.

St. Thomas Aquinas made theology the queen of all sciences and separated it from any mystical, experiential theology of union with the living God of Abraham, Isaac and Jacob. He taught theologians even into the 20th century that God cannot have a "real" relationship to us or any of His creatures.

> *God's temporal relations to creatures are in Him only because of our way of thinking of Him; but the opposite relation of creatures to him are realities in creatures.* [6]

The weakness of such an inherited "scholastic" theology lies in its inability to bring God into a personalized relationship with us in temporality and in matter. All too often, lesser theologians than St. Thomas pictured God as a "cosmic do-gooder," a "universal welfare agent." Western Christians, both Roman Catholic and Protestant, received Christianity through the framework of Augustinianism that was heavily characterized by a dualism which separated body from soul with an implicit denigration of anything material, including the human body.

Dr. Louis Dupré characterizes the loss of true transcendence in theology in these words:

> *From the sixteenth century on, however, reality became rapidly reduced to its objective, if not its physico-mathematical quality. The one-sidedness of the new approach seriously impaired the mind's self-understanding and, for the same reason, its ability to conceive a genuine transcendence. It even reduced our view of nature. What Heidegger writes about Descartes goes also for his successsors: the world turned into a presence-at-hand (Vorhanden), that is, an exclusive object of manipulation, closed to contemplation.* [7]

Human nature was too often viewed in Western Christianity as basically corrupt. Nature was no longer the place for creative work to build a better Christian world, but was separated in such thinking from God and from the spiritual world. Such a religious separation of God from nature made material nature a mere backdrop for human activity.

No wonder so many writers, such as Lynn White, Jr., have accused Western Christianity of justifying human authority over nature to exploit and rape it of its resources. He writes in his most influential essay: "The Historical Roots of Our Ecologic Crisis":

> *The greatest spiritual revolutionary in western history, St. Francis, proposed what he thought was an alternative Christian view of nature and man's relation to it; he tried to substitute the idea of the equality of all creatures, including man, for the idea of man's limitless rule of creation. He failed. Both our present science and our present technology are so tinctured with orthodox Christian arrogance toward nature that no solution for our ecologic crisis can be expected from them alone. Since the roots of our trouble are so largely religious, the remedy must also be essentially religious, whether we call it that or not. We must rethink and refeel our nature and destiny. The profoundly religious, but heretical sense of the primitive Franciscans for the spiritual autonomy of all parts of nature may point a direction. I propose Francis as a patron saint for ecologists.* [8]

MODERN INDUSTRIALIZATION

Three other factors caused greater separation of us human beings from the material nature around us.

The first is the development of the natural sciences and the beginning of technology that allowed scientists to discover universal laws and to control and manipulate nature as a mine to be exhausted of its hidden treasures and resources for the human race's greater "progress."

Nature came to be viewed, not so much as the theater of God's glory in which humanity is essentially embodied, but much more as a self-enclosed machine-like structure, set apart from both God and man, for the sake of domination.[9] Edwin A. Burtt describes the rise of this mechanical view of nature:

> . . . *The really important world outside was a world hard, cold, colorless, silent, and dead; a world of quantity, a world of mathematically computable motions in mechanical regularity. The world of qualities as immediately perceived by man became just a curious and quite minor effect of that infinite machine beyond.*[10]

Secondly, the philosophy of the Protestant German thinker, Immanuel Kant, had a great impact upon modern philosophy. Like Newton, Kant believed that nature is composed of immutable, hard, and dead conglomerations of moving particles.[11] He also separated God from the mechanical nature. God for Kant becomes that reality which is subjectively necessary for our practical or moral reason to postulate. God is totally transcendent and has no immediate immanence in objects of our experience. For Kant both God and man would remain in vital relationships, but both would have no relationship to nature. Protestantism would become highly "spiritualized" and would lose any prior ecological dimension.

But the main cause behind our modern ecological crisis must be directed to the forces of modern industrialism. Both liberal capitalism and Marxism, seeming enemies to each other, are henchmen to industrialization and exploiters of natural resources for economic gain. Lewis Mumford gives us this shrewd observation: "The power that was science and the power that was money were, in final analysis, the same kind of power: the power of abstraction, measurement, quantification."[12]

A TECHNOLOGICAL WORLD

Our technological world has produced many of the problems facing us today: water and air pollution; the pillage of mineral resources; the increasing list of extinct or endangered species of birds and animals; the far-reaching effect of pesticides; the wanton dumping of industrial chemicals on land and sea; the overwhelming accumulation of waste, garbage and junk; and especially the spiraling of the population explosion, all add up to an apocalyptic crisis.[13]

A concrete example is the massive mercury pollution found in Lake Erie, San Francisco Bay, the Delaware River, Lake Champlain and the Tennessee River. Mercury used in pulp mills and paper processing is absorbed from the water by plankton that is eaten by the fish. Fish are eaten by seals whose livers are used, ironically, as an iron supplement — a blood booster for humans! "You can just figure from this," said a biologist, "that there isn't any place in the whole world that isn't contaminated."[14]

Polluted air has increased lung disease across the nation to an alarming degree, to say nothing of an increase in cancer to all parts of the human body. The asphalt jungles filled with litter and dirt do violence to the people living in squalid tenement flats in a desert of isolation. They are cut off from any existential sense of unity and harmony with a fresh, new world of creation.

NON-TECHNOLOGICAL CULTURES

The early North American Indians and other members of non-technological societies lived in two worlds: that of the gods and that of primitive technology. Such non-scientific cultures found the numinous or God's sacred presence in all things. Such persons, living in a society that opened them to the sacred sense of the Absolute permeating all of nature, were easily bound to each other as brothers and sisters of the same Supreme Father and Mother of all. Such persons become receptors, not wishing to destroy, but to re-form or refashion.

Contrary to the Western Cartesian dichotomy that pits matter against spirit, body against soul, non-technological persons, like natural children in all cultures, are not compelled to *do* as to *be* within a living, dynamic flow of energy all around them, to be open and receptive to its creative power.

Yet we must not naively idealize such a non-scientific culture as desirable in all its aspects. The non-technological world lacks tools to take care of its growing population with the result that millions are undernourished and thousands die daily from starvation or diseases due to malnutrition. The passive, contemplative spirit had allowed diseases to go unchecked and mass land erosion to overtake such countries. Notwithstanding the reverence for trees, whole forests have been cut down for food and heating and never replaced, violating egregiously their principle of cosmic equilibrium.

A RETURN TO PARADISE

Where do we begin to develop an Earth spirituality? It is imperative that we see God's purpose in creating ourselves, the Earth and the entire universe. We have been living out our own human story or narrative of what we think reality is all about. We need to find an alternative myth to guide us into a oneness with God, with all human beings, with the living and non-living nature around us, with the entire universe.

Thomas Berry, in his beautiful and most important book, *The Dream of the Earth*, distinguishes between our culture and our genetic codings. Cultural coding is determined by free human choices within the context of a human community. When accepted, taught, lived by and handed down, especially through family and school education, such coding becomes the normative reference of reality and values for such a community.

We have already described the general cultural coding passed on for the past 300 years that, through science and technology and the economics of industrialization, has separated us from nature and created such frightening imbalances in our eco-systems. To change such a framework or *weltanschauung* and to acquire a new cultural coding, Berry insists that the creative power from any new, hologramic vision of human beings as a part of the Earth and all living and non-living creatures, is to be found in our genetic coding.

> *All these are means whereby we articulate our special mode of being and fulfill our role in the universal order of things, all in response to the spontaneities that emerge from our genetic coding; ultimately, of course, they emerge from the larger community of life, from the integral functioning of the planet Earth, from the comprehensive functioning of the universal order of things, and from the numinous source from which all things receive their being, their energy, and their inherent grandeur.* [15]

We need to establish a new cultural coding, an ecological coding that will educate all human beings into the inter-relatedness of all creatures in the universe. To do this, we need spiritual discipline and spiritual experiences to make contact through our genetic coding with the numinous and sacred presence of God, the unifying force through free, self-emptying love, present within our human unconscious and locked into the matrix of each atom and sub-atomic particle. It is through archetypes in the unconscious that we uncover knowledge never before known. Such knowledge is given to each human being, made by God according to His own image and likeness, to discover His Logos working creatively in all creatures and to respond joyfully and with spontaneity as a co-creator, as one working with the guiding Divine Logos.

It was from his unconscious that Einstein discovered the theory of relativity as a mystical experience of cosmic oneness, enfolded in the arms of the Divine Orderer in universal inter-relatedness of all things in the Source. His statement on this has already been quoted in Chapter One.

CALLED TO BE MYSTICS

Let us go to the beginning of creation to discover what God had in mind as His intention for creating this world. From God's revelation we see that before growing up to think almost exclusively with the conscious mind and suffering consequent separation from nature, early human beings lived in an Eden of perpetual childhood. They saw in dreams and spoke in poetry. The Book of Genesis pictures the first human beings walking through a garden-world like happy children, celebrating each day as though it were their first. All nature was an extension of themselves and they lived in the world like unborn children in the womb. At the same time they mothered and fathered the life growing around them, as they were mothered and fathered by the God they knew as intimately as they knew themselves.

All of us were created to be mystics, at home in heaven and on earth, drawing no line between the two. The first human beings took in the unified field of nature and spirit in one visionary glance and drank living water from the well of that Absolute Being we now call God. Adam and Jesus called this Being "Abba," or "Daddy," for they knew God as God was, not as the stranger our thinking, self-centered brains have created. Because they did not separate themselves from God or God from the world, these first human beings looked at creation and agreed with God that it was good. After the joyful harvest of their days, they danced, then slept and danced again, to the endless music of their dreams.

A poem written in Sanscrit five thousand years ago well described the Genesis story of our mystical oneness with God and all things created:

> . . . *Reach out beyond knowing and*
> *embrace oneness.*
> *Healing as you go, breathe the*
> *living word restoring creation.*
> *Share the spiritual fire and let the*
> *mystic light of God fill you to*
> *overflowing.*
> *Ultimately there is only one truth,*
> *one pure blessed reality:*
> *That the powers of love will pervade*
> *and overcome all things.*
> *We will rest in utter completion of*
> *wonder.*
> *We are not alone, but we are within*
> *the same mystical unfolding.*
> *Happy are we only in as far as*
> *kindness and vision live within*
> *shining outward.*
> *Words are shadows; acts are born of*
> *real caring and loving.*
> *A truth in stillness do we share in*
> *the moments beyond time,*
> *Fleeting touches of an ultimate*
> *total embrace.*
> *Within these things lies the most*
> *sacred and simple mystery of all:*
> *We are loved, utterly and*
> *completely.* [16]

All things belong to God, but we have taken them as ours, raping nature, taking it by force as something to be possessed and used for our own selfish purposes. Our technological control over nature had unleashed our demons into the world around us, and we live in fear of the fall-out from our own bombs. Toxic water and air sting the nose and rot the lungs. Public mineral resources are being handed over to the wealthy, impoverishing the rest of humankind.

Fumes from our machines rise up to cloud the atmosphere with a gaseous shroud that may eventually choke all plant, animal and human life on planet Earth. Noble human beings, created by God to be little less a god (Ps 8:5), become a quintessence of dust as we build up bigger walls to separate ourselves from others, the enemies who, we think, are out to destroy us. The real enemy, however, is that false self who gnaws at our insides until we are empty shells.

What was originally meant by God to have been a world both unending in its richness and diversity and a harmonious whole, unified by love, has been distorted into a world seen darkly through the glass of separation and alienation.

CREATING AN EARTH SPIRITUALITY

Such gigantic problems are not solved primarily by more technology or mere education, but by a better knowledge of our human relationship to earth, to other human beings and to ourselves individually. It is a question of creating a new set of values and a new system of ethics whereby we can guide our choices by principles beyond our own self-interest. What is needed is a new anthropology of man/woman as cosmic persons, citizens not just of America or even of Earth, but of the universe.

The communications media have opened up to us the possibility of being present to a fellow brother or sister in drought-stricken Africa. We have literally seen men walking on the moon and suddenly planetary distances do not exist as they did before. In a moment we can be present, in a psychic way, to the needs of everyone throughout the world.

But the greatest need and urgency for a change of values and a new ethics is to stop the pollution of ourselves interiorly. Saving the human race from isolation and alienation will not be done by mere negative motivation through fear of a final, cataclysmic war, but only if we begin to dispel the interior pollution of our inner spirits. This can come only in a newness of religious insight that all human beings are interdependent with each other but also with all created nature through a sense of community, of belonging and sharing together the riches that God has so abundantly given to us.

We need a new anthropology that builds an ethics, not based on our own individual rights so much as on our personal growth through personalistic relationships with all humans and with the very cosmos itself. Such a vision of the unity of interdependence of all nature can never be deduced from Euclidean axioms.

THE INWARD JOURNEY

Before we can discover in the macrocosm of the created world around us the unity of all things and the uniqueness of each individual creature in God's creative Word, we need to turn within ourselves. To transcend the limitations of science and human selfish interests over the rest of creation, we need to "inscend," in Thomas Berry's phrase, into our innermost self, hidden gold locked inside our darkened unconscious.

We need to move inwardly away from the noises we and the technological world create to foster even more damaging results against God's primeval unity of interrelatedness of all His creatures with each other and with Him. The poet Longfellow describes this movement inwardly to attain still-pointedness to hear God's Logos speaking to us:

Let us, then, labor for an inward
stillness and an inward healing;
That perfect silence where the lips
and heart
Are still, and we no longer
entertain
Our own imperfect thoughts and vain
opinions,
But God alone speaks in us, and we
wait
In singleness of heart, that we may
know
His will, and in silence of our
spirits,
That we may do His will, and do that
only.

Although God's sacred presence permeates all of creation, we human beings need to rediscover the sacred place within us. Teilhard de Chardin keenly describes the struggle within us to descend into this inner world which can be conquered only by faith in God's inner guidance:

We must try to penetrate our most secret self, and examine our being from all sides. Let us try, patiently, to perceive the ocean of forces to which we are subjected and in which our growth is, as it were, steeped. . . . I took the lamp and, leaving the zone of everyday occupations and relationships where everything seems clear, I went down into my inmost self, to the deep abyss whence I feel dimly that my power of action emanates. But as I moved further and further away from the conventional certainties by which social life is superficially illuminated, I became aware that I was losing contact with myself. At each step of the descent a new person was disclosed within me of whose name I was no longer sure, and who no longer obeyed me. And when I had to stop my exploration because the path faded from beneath my steps, I found

a bottomless abyss at my feet. . . . At that moment . . . I felt the
distress characteristic of a particle adrift in the universe, the
distress which makes human wills founder daily under the crush-
ing number of living things and stars. And if someone saved me,
it was hearing the voice of the Gospel . . . speaking to me, from the
depth of the night: It is I, be not afraid. [17]

OUR INNER SELF

One great temptation in today's world of gimmicks and practical do-it-yourself gadgets is that we can discover and awaken to
ever-increasing intensity our inner self by some quick method. We
see this danger in Westerners studying methods from the Far-
Eastern religions without any understanding of the ''story'' that
goes with such techniques.

This is to forget that the inner self is not a compartment of our
being. It is characterized primarily as a spontaneity, and this
necessitates our growth into greater personal freedom. We must
move away from our cultural codings that have kept us all too often
locked into an alienation from our true self that is basically societal
and at-oneness with all other creatures. Our inner self is a process
of continued growth that involves our whole being and long years
of inner discipline and prayer.

To journey inwardly and to touch the sacredness of both God
as the Ground of our being and the sacredness of our true selves in
His creative Word and the sacred oneness we have with all of God's
creation demands a dying process unto new life. It is the seed that
falls into the earth and apparently dies, only to blossom forth in an
unfolding of inner power commanding greater life. So our inner
life in touching the sacred within awakens to a new awareness of a
more total and unified existence. When it is stirred, it communicates a new life to our intelligence, so that we reflectively and
consciously live on a deeper level. This awareness is not a thing we

possess. It is a state of being whereby we *are*. It is a real, indefinable experience of new living relationships of an *I* to the *Thou* of God, to other human persons and to an energized, personalized world.

This experience of the inner self cannot be put into a conceptualized "box." It is not a "thing," and hence there is no trick, no method, no "meditation" alone that can cajole it out of its hiding. A disciplined asceticism can only bring about the proper climate in which the inner self may both be recognized and be rendered more present. This climate produced by a spiritual regime includes such things as silence, poverty and detachment, purity of heart and indifference.

In every experience, whether religious, moral or artistic, that opens itself to the transcendent and spiritual world, there is some expansion of our inner self. Such a transcendent, spiritual experience takes on more and more beauty and meaningfulness accompanied by a certain incommunicability from the active participation of the inner self.

True contemplation should never be considered as something given only to exceptionally talented psychic mystics. Contemplation is the state of living immanently in the depths of our being and there, through the infusion of God's Spirit of the gifts of faith, hope and love, to grow in ever-expanding consciousness that the Trinity abides there and dynamically energizes us by God's love.

OUTWARD JOURNEY
INTO THE CREATED WORLD

The closer we touch God in our heart, the closer we are also drawn to a union of love toward our neighbors and toward all of God's creation. St. Dorotheus of the 6th century used the example of a wheel. The closer the spokes of the wheel move to the center, the closer they come to each other. The further they move out from the center, the more distance separates one spoke from another.

Thomas Merton well describes this universal sense of "oneness" with all others through silent immersion in God:

> *It is in fact the function of solitude to make one realize such things with a clarity that would be impossible to anyone completely immersed in the other cares, the other illusions, and all the automatisms of a tightly collective existence. . . . It is because I am one with them that I owe it to them to be alone, and when I am alone they are not "they" but my own self. There are no strangers!*[18]

Such authentic human beings — who are continually growing in their true self before their personalized Ground of Being — grow in all human situations to become still more one in loving openness and service with all their "brothers and sisters," embracing all living and non-living creatures in love that differentiates as it unites.

True growth in authentically becoming a human person must be measured by this oneness with the Earth and all of God's creatures. Chief Seattle, leader of the Native American Suquamish tribe in the 19th century, summarized this truth:

> *This we know. The earth does not belong to man; man belongs to the earth. This we know. All things are connected like blood which unites one family. All things are connected. Whatever befalls the earth befalls the sons of the earth. Man did not weave the web of life; he is merely a strand in it. Whatever he does to the web, he does to himself.*[19]

The world, therefore, from God's viewpoint is one. All creatures, through the creative inventiveness and synergism of human beings working with God, are meant to be inter-related in a harmonious wholeness. Each part has its proper place within the whole universe. Each creature depends on and gives support to all the others in one great body, all of which has been created in and through God's Word (cf. Psalm 104).

For such human beings in their oneness with all creatures through their grounding in the absolute Sacred at the heart of matter, to recklessly destroy any part of God's material creation is to harm oneself. For to destroy a living species is to silence a part of God's voice in our universe. God's Logos in whom all things are created will no longer speak to us about God's beauty and loving presence in such creatures.

Pope John Paul II in his recent encyclical *On Social Concern* expresses our need to acquire:

> . . . *a growing awareness of the fact that one cannot use with impunity the different categories of beings, whether living or inanimate — animals, plants, the natural elements — simply as one wishes, according to one's own economic needs. On the contrary, one must take into account the nature of each being and of its natural connection in an ordered system, which is precisely the 'cosmos' (article 34).*

No longer can we read God's injunction in the Book of Genesis (1:28) as an invitation to conquer nature by exploiting His gifts to us through selfish motives, but with a serious faith-response to become true stewards who protect, nurture and develop all hidden potentialities within nature, since all is sacred. Christians should will — in the spirit of St. Benedict's spirituality, through interaction with the material world — to love in God's real, existential world and thus adoringly work to build all things into a oneness with Christ unto God's eternal glory.

WE ARE
THE CONSCIOUSNESS OF THE UNIVERSE

To build a new spirituality of our relationships with God through our relationships with the material world around us, we must move in an ever-expanding consciousness of the unity that binds all of God's creation together. Technology has given us a world that is expanding in riches at a tremendous rate. We must not, in our most pessimistic moods, think that urban life and the world of technology are evil in themselves and lie outside of God's eternal plan.

We expand in our consciousness precisely by accepting responsibility for shaping new forms of life and reality in accordance with right reason. We are the lever lifting up a brute world by our creative and faithful activity. We are the "consciousness" and the "enspiriting" of the material world, drawing out the latent heights and depths of the evolutionary process of all things in Christ, as St. Paul teaches in his letters to the Ephesians and Colossians.

The more awakened is our consciousness to its ultimate direction, the greater the moral precision in our individual life. Such precision and direction are linked with our guiding values that we call our ethics. Such values emanate from the core of our habitual convictions, illuminating attitudes about our lives and the ultimate meaning of existence which goes far beyond mere expediency or exploitation of the world around us. Increasing perception and sensitivity, then, attunes us to an increasing radius of goodness and evil, inviting freedom of choice in a widening horizon.

FORWARD — AN ONGOING GENESIS

We have seen that to develop an Earth spirituality we need to journey inward to discover the source of our creativity in touching the immanent God at the center of our being. As we become healed through contact with the Sacred, we reach out in a creative and unifying way to the world around us. The third element in a new earth consciousness is to journey forward to create a new cosmos. Evolution has a built-in movement always toward greater complexity and yet greater conscious unity.

It is a dynamic call to become a fully realized person, a call to freedom and love. We respond to a community of persons interrelated to each other as well as to the whole material creation surrounding us by fashioning in union with God's Spirit the whole into a greater personalistic community. We are very much, along with the whole of creation, caught up within the historical process.

But history unfolds through our free and loving creative response to the living community around us, both human and subhuman. Community calls for a super-consciousness and super-loving which leads to a super-becoming. To be moral and truly religious we must discover our places and roles in the totality of the whole evolution of the world.

All created beings are tied together in their thrust toward fulfillment. Natures of created beings can no longer be considered in the tight compartments of Aristotelian metaphysics, as static, self-contained forms. All matter is rushing in a "forward" and at the same time in an "upward" movement toward the Spirit. Natures are not only apt for receiving a "supernatural" ingrafting, but they present themselves as "supernaturalizable" in the divine decree and activity, creating and bringing them to their completion with our human and free cooperation. Divinity already shoots through all of creation with uncreated energies of love, if we only had the eyes to see!

Thus our forward journey starts with the present historical situation with all its tensions and threatening forces. This cannot be the end, for that lies ahead in a hoped-for better future. We are not yet what we can become. Nor is the entire universe static and locked into a Sartrean "no-exit." We human beings are called by God's Spirit to bring order from chaos, harmony where there is discord, peace and love where there is conflict and hatred. Through contemplation and action, as we become a more authentic human community, we can build a more human universe-community. Our meaningfulness lies in building a better world through transcending our own self-interests in order to live for the larger community of which we are the reflecting agent.

SELF-TRANSCENDENCE

Victor Frankl discovered the dynamics of true human actualization in a Nazi concentration camp. He wrote after his experiences there:

Human existence is essentially self-transcendence rather than self-actualization. Self-actualization is not a possible aim at all, for the simple reason that the more a man would strive for it, the more he would miss it. For only to the extent to which man commits himself to the fulfillment of his life's meaning, to this extent he also actualizes himself. In other words, self-actualization cannot be attained if it is made an end in itself, but only as a side effect of self-transcendence. [20]

NEEDED: A NEW MYTH OF CREATION

We are in need of a new myth or story to guide us in our forward journey. We reject any literal interpretation of the story in the Book of Genesis that God created the entire universe in six days! The final end of the universe is all too often conceived by Christians as a ''deus ex machina,'' totally independent of human co-creation when the world will end with the sudden second coming of the Risen One to take us ''redeemed'' souls out of an annihilated world.

As we search for a new narrative to guide us into the far future, we also see the inadequacies of the modern evolutionist story associated with the work of Charles Darwin. In the Darwinian view, creation is a lengthy, slow process evolving over millions of years. Human beings appear at a later stage with the evolution of higher primates. But the inadequacies of this theory lie in the vehement rejection of God as the sacred, inner Orderer, moving all to an unending growth in a world community of intimate love.

Such a view denies any hope beyond a certain point of evolution if all ends in death and annihilation. Teilhard de Chardin, one of many "new age" thinkers, presents us with a new, creative synthesis of what has already been found in the writings of St. John, St. Paul and the early Eastern Fathers. He calls us to rediscover the whole inward history of creation, the evolution of human consciousness based on the principle that with greater complexity of matter there is a concomitant history of inwardness of greater consciousness which brings about greater inter-relatedness among all beings.

Creation is reconceived by Teilhard out of God's revelation in the light of evolution as an unfinished process. Salvation history and creation history go together. This means that redemption and salvation take place only in our role as co-creators with God in a world that is continuously *becoming* as we human beings respond in loving obedience to co-create according to God's Logos, His Divine Word in whom all things come into being.

A new global spirituality must be seen as a creative spirituality that moves toward cooperative participation in the divine creative work. Now holiness means the activating of our human creative energies in the service of evolving the universe into greater consciousness. Redemption still is a vital part of bringing about a new creation in a synergism with the divine energies, since we cannot heal ourselves of our selfish resistances without God's graces.

In this thoroughly Christian view, the meaninglessness of creative human beings and an evolving universe before death is overcome by Christian hope in the victory of the Risen One, now inserted more marvelously into the creation process by His resurrectional presence living in His members.

The final goal of the creative process in the universe is the appearance of the Kingdom of God. This is characterized by a maximum development of consciousness. This must be measured by an increased socialization into a unified community with heightened individuation or uniqueness of each member. The final future of God's plan of creation has to manifest a final intensity of communion and personal fulfillment "when God will be all in all" (1 Cor 15:28).[21]

CHRISTOGENESIS

If divine-human communion is the end of creation, then the creation of such a communion is the way to that end. Such a cosmic creation spirituality will also be a transforming, unitive or mystical spirituality, for only by building the communion now in an evolving *cosmogenesis* and an *anthropogenesis*, to use Teilhard's terms,[22] can the appearance of the truly "new age" appear. It will be the biblical Kingdom of God or the phase of *Christogenesis.*

The full appearance of the cosmos as *christic* will take place when God ". . . would bring everything together under Christ, as head, everything in the heavens and everything on earth" (Ep 1:10). The basis of such future unification must be love-energy, the unitive energy binding the human community together, as it also brings about personalization.

Therefore, a new global spirituality must effect two things. It must be a guiding light to us pilgrims journeying on planet Earth. This enlightenment comes about through an effective vision and a new consciousness. Vision creates energy, both ethical and affective. Other visions, such as Darwinism and Marxism, fail to transcend the death-barrier. Hence they cannot bring forth the necessary energy to attain a self-transcending goal.

Only God, who is immortal and immanently present in material creatures as uncreated energies of love, can overcome the death-barrier and also provide the creative love-energy for human beings to co-direct the world toward its final goal.[23] God communicates meaningfulness that culminates in intimate communion between Himself and us through His Word. The Word made flesh, Jesus Christ, by His dying on the cross, having been raised up in glory by His Father in the resurrection and releasing His Holy Spirit in our hearts, can now be recognized by us as the source of energy that unites all things into a living organism that is nothing less than the Body of Christ.

We must turn to God's Word, the Logos, in the next chapter to be enlightened by Him guiding us. He loves us so passionately as to have self-emptied Himself in death, so that we can live forever in our oneness with Him by now working with His energies of love to energize the entire universe. One with Him, we can turn the universe and ourselves and Christ included back to the Father so that ''there is only Christ: he is everything and he is in everything'' (Col 3:11).

An apt summary and conclusion to this chapter on Earth spirituality is this quotation from Teilhard de Chardin that calls for our continued reflection and a life-time of acting according to its wisdom:

> *To adore formerly meant preferring God to things, by referring them back to Him and sacrificing them for Him. To adore now has come to mean pledging oneself body and soul to creative act, by associating oneself with it so as to bring the world to its fulfillment by effort and research. Loving one's neighbor formerly meant not defrauding him and binding up his wounds. Charity, from now on, while not ceasing to be imbued with compassion,*

will find its fulfillment in a life given for common advance. Being pure formerly meant, in the main, standing aside and preserving oneself from stain. Tomorrow chastity will call, above all, for a sublimation of powers of flesh and of all passion. Being detached formerly meant not concerning oneself with things and only taking from them the least possible. Being detached now means step-by-step moving beyond all truth and beauty by power of the very love that one bears for them. Being resigned, formerly could signify passive acceptance of present conditions of the universe. Being resigned now will no longer be allowed, save to the warrior fainting away in the arms of the angel. [24]

3

A Logos Mysticism

In order to prepare for writing this
book, I felt the need to dialogue with a selected group of persons
whom I knew as ones eagerly seeking to advance to deeper levels of
consciousness. I composed a letter with three questions and sent it
out to 135 unsuspecting men and women of various walks of life. I
asked them, in brief, to describe how they saw the present movement of the Spirit in creating a Christian New Age consciousness;
what desired elements of such planetary consciousness did they
believe were emerging in the past thirty years that they felt would
continue into the 21st century; and how were they individually
contributing to create such a New Age consciousness?

I was gratefully humbled by the 65% who took time and some
pain to respond to my questions. A few wondered why I was
getting caught up in this New Age thinking! The majority con-
curred in general with the tenor of a dear friend's response. In my
eyes he is an outstanding modern mystic, who through his lectures
and books has been a leader for several decades in promoting a new
Christian consciousness.

He sees this movement in its best aspects as a movement of the
Holy Spirit in newness of creation and renewal by re-creation of old
forms of thought and religious beliefs. The two characteristics of

New Age consciousness are, for him, 1) the personal experience of the divine Life-breath within us; and 2) the synergy of our human creativity with the Source of life and constant renewal of life's forms. ''The movement is away from fragmentation toward wholeness. It is our responsibility to give ourselves to that movement of the Spirit towards ever more complex, ever more comprehensive unity, a dying to the old when no longer viable, and the bringing forth of the new that begets new life.''

PERIODS OF CONSCIOUSNESS-TRANSITIONS

I believe anyone who is in touch with what is happening around our globe is convinced that we are witnessing a radical transformation, or at least a call to decide to move into a transition to a higher human consciousness. Dr. Karl Jaspers, in his work *The Origin and Goal of History*,[1] outlines three great transitions in the emergence of human consciousness. His schema will give us a perspective from which we can see more clearly the nature of what is happening as we move into the new millennium.

1) Jaspers uses the term ''axial period'' to refer to the first great breakthrough in human consciousness that took place in the centuries between 2000 B.C. to 800 B.C. It is the *axis* that gave birth to everything which since then we human beings have been able to be.[2]

The move in greater consciousness was away from the mythic to self-reflective thinking, from fusion with the cosmos and the tribe to independent, individual identity which is distanced, even alienated, from nature and the collectivity. At this time the great religions were genuinely born and our fundamental categories of thought arose: In China with Confucius and Lao-tzu, in India with Gautama Buddha, in Persia with Zoroaster, in Greece with Thales, Pythagoras, Socrates and Plato, and in Israel with the prophetic movement. Jaspers does not deny that Jesus belonged to this period: "From an historical viewpoint Jesus was the last in the series of Jewish prophets and stood in conscious continuity to them."[3]

John Cobb characterizes this first axial transition into greater human consciousness as rationality breaking forth to become more dominant in the human psychic life.[4] It brought the ability to control, check and even to overturn mystical thinking, governed by projecting, fantasy and wish fulfillment. The outstanding feat is the new sense of what it means to be an individual and not merely to belong to a tribe or to be undifferentiated from the rest of created nature without any uniqueness. The same "I" is grasped as the "doer" in the past, present and future, who is responsible for his/her actions toward other persons and material creatures.

2) The second transition made possible by the first is the beginning and development from the 18th century to present times of our technological and scientific age. The great danger of this further development of the first axial age is, as we have pointed out, that it threatens global existence with cataclysmic destruction by restricting our human personhood to being a scientific observer of a world of objects, suited only for exploitation.

3) We are entering now into a *Second Axial Period*, which is bringing about a global consciousness with an awareness that all human beings and all material creatures are inter-related in a unity in richest diversity through our human effort to responsibly create such a new world. Here we see no evolution infallibly bringing us into such a loving community without our free choice. Rather than an enforced, inescapable evolution into such a unity, we must view this stage of planetary oneness as a challenge to all human beings to bring about such loving unity through creative service to the whole world.

ROLE OF CHRISTIANITY

The central point of this book is to see from Christianity's viewpoint how Christians can participate in this *Second Axial Period*. What is so unique about this transition into greater human consciousness is that it represents the summation of the cosmic levels of consciousness from the mythic age, through the *First Axial Period* of human individuation. Thus it is bringing about a unity with the world around us as was common in the mythic stage, but which preserves the subjective, reflective consciousness of the *First Axial Period*.

With the breakdown of the Church's cultural dominance in the Western industrialized world, we Christians need to go back to our roots, to our traditions, and sift out the cultural baggage of previous ages in order to retain the seeds of eternal truths of God's revelation to the human race.

We urgently need to articulate such truths in ways by which we can live them in the context of the planetary consciousness that is taking place around us in our modern society. We need to see that Christianity can work with a developing world, no longer maintaining its triumphalism of the two swords of Pope Boniface VIII, a jurisdiction of the Church over the Kingdom of Heaven and also over the temporal kingdoms of this world, but becoming a humble co-worker with all human societies to bring this world into a new creation.

VATICAN COUNCIL II

Pope John XXIII, who convoked the ecumenical council of Vatican II in 1962, wanted to bring about a new Pentecost. He wished to open the windows and doors of the Vatican and let a powerful wind of the Spirit blow out the stagnant air and dust covering so many Catholic institutions and beliefs and practices.

In the great Constitutions of the Council *On the Church, On Revelation, On Liturgy,* and the decrees *On Ecumenism, On Religious Life, On the Eastern Churches, On the Laity* and *On the Missions* as well as the *Declaration On Non-Christian Religions,* but especially in the Pastoral Constitution *On the Church in the Modern World* and the *Declaration On Religious Freedom,* we find a new and promising openness to cultures and religions other than the Roman Catholic form of Christianity, an openness to appraise positively the trends and movements at work today in the City of human beings. There is an openness to the advance in history and the social and psychological sciences.

The Catholic Church is putting itself consciously at the service of the family of human beings, regardless of race or creed. In a word, there is a desire to engage in a true dialogue with the world, especially in the ministry of service to the human race. The children of God receive freedom as a gift from the Father through Christ in the Holy Spirit to develop it within the Church, but also within the world, always for both the sake of the world and the Church.

GOD COMMUNICATES THROUGH HIS WORD

Let us explore a *Logos Mysticism* that, when properly conceived in terms of a process of interpersonal relationships between the personalized triune community of love we call God and all of God's creation, will be the foundation-stone for a true dialogue between religion and science.

I would like to frame this important religious concept that God seeks personally to communicate Himself to His created world, especially to and through His human children whom He made according to His own image and likeness (Gn 1:26-27), around a very suggestive painting. At Goleta, California, in the Newman Chapel of the University of California at Santa Barbara, a unique and provocative mural dominates the wall behind the altar. The artist, Michael Dvortsak, based his work on Teilhard de Chardin's belief that, since the Word became flesh and lived among us, "Christ invests Himself organically with the very majesty of His universe." He has sought to draw out in dramatic, pictorial form the implications of the Incarnation in language that students studying at a modern university would understand.

Christ is depicted with arms outstretched, in a crucified form. In a circular movement pouring down from one hand and up to the other are the vivid symbols of a living world, that of the inner space of the submicroscopic and that of outer space, of the macrocosm, of planets and galaxies and quasars.

Christ looks down with intense interest and spiritual concern toward every created atom. The artist stresses the unity of the whole created universe in Christ, who has taken on matter and is "inside" the universe, creating, developing, and divinizing it until all is brought back in glory to the Father. It is an artistic profession of the faith proclaimed by St. Paul: ". . . for in him were created all things in heaven and on earth, everything visible and everything invisible" (Col 1:16).

The whole life cycle is shown to come forth from Christ, through Him and in Him, starting with the individual unicell of life, to the union of sperm and ovum, to the formation of the foetus. From the mountains and valleys making up man's complicated inner, physical world, to the planets and galaxies of outer space, all things sweep out and down in the shape of a human heart from the head of Christ, back up from the bottom through the figure of Christ.

The artist is showing us that God loves His creation. The world is full of vibrant energy, God's own concerned, loving activity through the Incarnate Word. The Body of Christ is being formed by the matter of this universe as each atom is brought by human beings, the contemplatives, under the power of Christ's Spirit. God loves the world that is of His making. It is good, and He is involved in its future. He is present in it as an inner force, making it evolve; He lives for it; dies for it. There is hope for this wildly careening universe, because there is a principle of harmony at its center. This principle is Christ the Evolver; Christ the Logos.

AN ORDERED LOVE

The Trinity, absolute inaccessibility, self-contained in its inner perfection, still seeks, as part of this perfection, to pour itself out in order that its Goodness may be shared. The "otherness" of the created world, its "worldliness," insofar as it is not God, is ultimately its only way of existing. Because we are created distinct from God, in His love for us and in His desire to share His love with us, we possess the possibility of growth. And growth means life and love.

Christ is the Word, the Logos, through whom God speaks to us, and in that Speech we have our being. Reality is not out of our own finite human minds nor from our own human words. True reality flows out of God through His creative Word in His Spirit of love. The abyss between God and nothingness is spanned through the Logos. He is the reason why we exist and why the entire world is being created and given into our hands. We are called to make our awesome response to the Giver of life by becoming co-creators with God the Creator.

We cannot be united with God to reach our fulfillment unless God gives Himself to us through communication unto communion. "God's love for us was revealed when God sent into the world his only Son so that we could have life through him" (1 Jn 4:9). St. Paul clearly shows us the plan of God's creation: "We are God's work of art, created in Christ Jesus to live the good life as from the beginning he meant us to live it" (Ep 2:10).

When God's Logos assumed flesh, our humanity, when He took upon Himself matter, as eternally ordained by God in the total plan of creation, we and the entire material world were irrevocably assumed into that hypostatic union. As divinity and humanity were joined into one being "without confusion," as the Council of Chalcedon (451 A.D.) described the hypostatic union, so by analogy we and the world are joined together with divinity without confusion or assimilation, but in a unity of love and individuated uniqueness of each of us creatures of God.

The human nature of Christ, living united with His divinity for all eternity, will always remain His glorified humanity. So too this created world will come into its fullness precisely by entering into a conscious relationship of love with God through His Son, the Logos enfleshed by His Spirit. Christ is acting within the evolving process of this world to allow the world to be itself and to let each of us become our true selves in the creative Logos-made-flesh, Jesus Christ.

MODERN MYSTICS

Regardless of whatever culturally conditioned theological and philosophical vehicles were employed in interpreting the Christian message, mystics, universally and throughout the centuries of Christianity, have moved within the context of a dynamic and developmental process of the unfolding of the God-human-world relationships.

As modern mystics are led progressively into the inner meaning of reality, they are not led away from the created world, but rather are led into reverence and worship of God as present everywhere within the created world. The flowers, the trees, birds, animals, the beauties of each new season, the sun, moon, stars, the mountains, lakes oceans; the whole world reveals to the contemplatives the loving presence of God, concerned to give Himself actively and creatively to us human beings in His many gifts. God is contemplated as an almighty Transcendence that is the Source and Sustainer of all created life.

Mystics in our modern world are being called to enter even deeper into reality as they adore the presence of God as the One who "contains" the created world and gives it its "consistency." As Paul preached to the Athenians, our God ". . . is not far from any of us, since it is in him that we live and move and exist. . ." (Ac 17:28). We are not alone. God is everywhere, present and actively concerned to move us into greater oneness with Him.

Modern mystics breathe and realize in their very breath and in the breath infused into every living being that it is the uncreated energies of God which give human beings and our world the capacity to evolve into children of God. Creation for the mystic is an ongoing process. Whatever is, can become a point of meeting God the Doer, the almighty and loving force energizing the universe.

Above all, we find within ourselves a special sharing in God's energies in our power to know God personally and to love and surrender ourselves to Him. Thus the mystic can no longer be content with merely adoring the beautiful, harmonious presence of God in His universe. The mystics surrender themselves in their own unique energies to those of God. A new communion of love is reached as we seek to "do", not according to our inner words and desires, but according to God's Word. Our impulsiveness and self-centeredness now change to active receptivity in our openness to cooperate with the graceful energies of God, operating at each moment in each event.

Such modern mystics respond to this presence of God acting in all creatures by returning love through their loving activities. They submit their whole being, especially their intellectual and volitional powers, to the indwelling Trinity, Father, Son and Holy Spirit. They do this in order, in the words of St. Paul, to become Christ's "ambassadors" and "reconcilers" of the whole universe back to the Father (2 Cor 5:18-20).

Above all, such enlightened persons pierce through the illusory values that pamper the senses, that exalt the independence of a self-centered existence, in order to arrive at a faith-vision that actively allows themselves to "suffer" with God suffering in the world. They see God's loving hand in the "pruning" of the vine branch in order to bring forth more fruit. By total death to self there is effected gradually a more perfect union with God and with each creature, especially with other human beings. Rather than running away from the world, the modern mystic is now totally at God's disposition to work in oneness with His Logos to bring the world into its greater spiritual, conscious existence, into a greater unity of love.

THE CROSS LEADS TO RESURRECTION

Far from being an easy mysticism, encouraging a sickening quietism or a self-love that equates the individual human being with God, such a vision of prayer is at the heart of the Christian message of the cross leading to the resurrection. There is a transformation of the universe to the degree that we human beings, cooperators with God's activity, die to our own views and values and lovingly and trustingly submit in surrender to the inner power of God's Spirit, revealing through God's Logos His plan of harmony. This vision of deeper prayer will always stand as the essential characteristic separating a Logos mysticism from all other forms of mystical oneness with the Absolute.

PSYCHOLOGY OF A LOVING PRESENCE

To build a true Christian Logos mysticism, we must first understand how love in God and in ourselves is always a communicating presence of the gift of oneself to another toward ever-increasing union of an *I-Thou* intimacy. When we love another, we become a gifted presence to the other. We want to live in union with that person so as to be a conscious presence as gift as often as possible, not only physically in space and time, but more importantly in the inner recesses of our consciousness.

However, we become present to each other in deeper and deeper consciousness to the degree that we can share our most intimate thoughts through speech. Words are the most ordinary way of communicating our inner selves as gift to the other. Without internal words that can be expressed in externalized words, spoken or written or acted out in gestures, we would never grow in love and greater union with God and other persons.

And we are this way as self-communicating beings, because God is this way in His essence as Love. God the Father, in absolute silence, in a communication of love impossible for human beings to understand, speaks His one eternal Word through His Spirit of love. In that one Word, the Father is perfectly present, totally self-giving to His Son. "In him lives the fullness of divinity" (Col 2:9).

But in His Spirit, the Father also hears His Word come back to Him in a perfect, eternal "yes" of total surrendering love that is again the Holy Spirit. The Trinity is a reciprocal community of a movement of the Spirit of love between Father and Son. Our weak minds cannot fathom the peace and joy, the ardent excitement and exuberant self-surrender that flow in a reposeful motion between Father and Son through the Holy Spirit. The Father becomes real only because He can communicate in love with His Word. His Word gives Him His identity as Father, but that means eternal self-giving to the Other, His Word in love.

GOD'S WORD IN CREATION

If God's essence is love (1 Jn 4:8), He seeks by His nature to share His being by communicating His presence. In the Judeo-

Christian tradition, God becomes a God-toward-others by communicating Himself through His Word and His Spirit of Love. God
creates the whole world as good; or, better, He is always creating it
as a sign of His burning desire to give Himself in faithful communication through His Word. The world at its interior is filled with the
self-communicating Trinity. God is filling the universe with His
loving Self. His uncreated energies swirl through and fill all creatures with His loving, creative presence.

> *Yahweh's love fills the earth.*
> *By the word of Yahweh the heavens*
> *were made, their whole arrays by the*
> *breath of his mouth.*
> *. . . He spoke, and it was created;*
> *he commanded and there it stood*
> *(Ps 33:5-9).*

God's creative Word, the Logos, is personified in the Old
Testament as Wisdom itself. God delights to give Himself through
His Word to His creatures.

> *. . .when he laid down the foundations*
> *of the earth,*
> *I was by his side, a master craftsman,*
> *delighting him day after day,*
> *ever at play in his presence,*
> *at play everywhere in his world,*
> *delighting to be with the sons of*
> *men (Pr 8:29-31).*

Everything flows out of God's exuberant fullness of being and
becomes a reality in His communicating Word. He speaks through
His Word and oceans and mountains, birds and beasts, flowers and
all living things spring into being under His laughing, joyful gaze.

Nothing that is can escape His loving touch, His presence as Giver of life (Ps 139:1-3; Jr 23:24).

Not only does God communicate Himself in creation, but He is a sustaining, directing God. He brings forth His presence through His communicating Word that is locked in His creation, but only if we human beings are there to discover God at the heart of matter.

CREATION OF HUMAN BEINGS

Yet the millions of creatures do not image God's tremendous passion to communicate Himself more perfectly, even to be in communion, the most intimate union with His created human beings. From all eternity, God's Word spoken in all of creation was only as a means in order that this outpouring God could be present to one unique creation: men and women.

The care and concern in this more perfect step of self-giving through His Word can be seen in the account of Genesis. God is seen as a self-communicating community, freely deciding on a new course of creative giving:

> *God said, 'Let us make man in our own image, in the likeness of ourselves, and let them be masters of the fish of the sea, the birds of heaven, the cattle, all the wild beasts and all the reptiles that crawl upon the earth.' God created man in the image of himself, in the image of God he created him, male and female he created them (Gn 1:26-27).*

DIGNITY OF WOMAN AND MAN

We human beings, of all God's material creatures, possess an intrinsic relationship to the triune community. By possessing an intellect and will, we are able in freedom to posit ourselves, each of us, as an *I*, dependent on the Absolute *I* of God.

The Protestant theologian, Emil Brunner, captures the patristic understanding of our human relationships to the Image-Word of God:

> *God created man in such a way that in this very creation man is summoned to receive the Word actively, that is, he is called to listen, to understand and to believe. God creates man's being in such a way that man knows that he is determined and conditioned by God, and in this fact is truly human. The being of man as an "I" is being from and in the Divine "Thou," or, more exactly, from and in the Divine Word, whose claim 'calls' man's being into existence. . . . The characteristic imprint of man, however, only develops on the basis of Divine determination as an answer to a call, by means of a decision. The necessity for decision, an obligation which he can never evade, is the distinguishing feature of man . . . it is the being created by God to stand 'over-against' Him who can reply to God, and who in this answer alone fulfills — or destroys — the purpose of God's creation.* [6]

God would communicate Himself to His human children through His Word and He would progressively give Himself to them as He gives Himself to His own Word. God walks with man and woman and dialogues with them in the cool of the day; a picture of peace and repose and harmony in God's Logos (Gn 2:8, 15).

SIN: DEAFNESS TO GOD'S WORD

Sin entered to disrupt this familiarity between God and human beings. Sin is an act whereby we humans close our spiritual ears of conscience to God's Word. We no longer want to be present in obedience to His Word that speaks only words of dynamic unifying love.

We were meant in God's designs to be open and docile to His Word. The first step in realizing our potential as truly human beings in vital, conscious communication and communion with God is to be like virgin earth. God's Word would fall gently upon the softness of our hearts and take root there. Yet our first parents and all succeeding ancestors of ours, and ourselves included, rejected the call to be receptive and obedient, gentle and open to God's communicating Word. We yielded to the temptation to become powerful like God (Gn 3:5) so we could rule our lives in complete independence. We wanted to make our own words the source of all creative reality.

Through sin, we began our long pilgrimage in exile, absent to the community of God's personalized love of Father, Son and Spirit. We are not present, therefore, to our true logos or true self in God's creative Logos. Yet God continually speaks His Word. God is present, touching us in millions of ways, yet we fail to hear His Word speak to us and effect a loving communication toward an intimate communion between ourselves and the Trinity.

COVENANT PEOPLE

Yet God, in His mercy, chose one man, Abraham, to be the father of His People. Because Abraham believed in God and obeyed His Word faithfully, he was justified, for to such, God would again reveal His loving presence (Gn 17:2-8). Through Isaac and Jacob and the twelve sons of Jacob, God began to fashion His new People. He speaks His Word from the burning bush to Moses. His Word is a revelation of a God who is concerned in His actions with the happiness of His People.

God's heart, imaged by the burning bush (Ex 3:9-10) is on fire with love for His People. God is touched by their sufferings. The Immutable bends down and suffers thirst, hunger and oppression along with His suffering People. God is not a static noun, but a living, active verb and a preposition. He is "Ehyeh Aser Ehyeh" (Ex 3:13), which means, not merely: "I am who I am," but more: "I am Yahweh who will become your God in the next step. I am with you always." A loving God is always moving toward His children. His Word (*Dabar* in Hebrew) is a dynamic concept, totally dependent on God who communicates His Word to us human beings. *Word* in the Hebraic sense possesses a *dianoetic* content. *Word* in Scripture presents the reader with a thought whereby a thing is known through a concept. The inner nature of God, the end of our lives, our own human nature, can be known through the revealed Word.

But there is also another element in *Dabar*, which is the dynamic power the *word* releases in the receiver of the word. The word is charged with creative power and energy that flow from the word into the receiver, transforming the listener somewhat into the word and also the mind speaking the word.[7]

God speaks His Word to Moses in the Tent of the Meeting (Ex 33:7-11). He speaks His Word from the Ark of the Covenant carried among His desert People and became a protective power, freeing His People from the attacks of enemies, bringing food, fresh water and guidance to them in any and all of their needs. He speaks to His People through His chosen Prophets, who became God's special carriers of His Word revealed to His People, especially in the exile period.

God's Word is Wisdom, a Spirit which loves human beings and educates them as to the right path to holiness (Ws 1:5-6). But God dwells and communicates Himself through His Word in the Temple on Mt. Zion in Jerusalem. To go into the Temple of Jerusalem and dwell there all the days of one's life, to gaze on Yahweh's holiness and loveliness in that blessed sanctuary becomes the cry, not only of the Psalmist (Ps 84:1-2, 4-5, 10), but of every believing Jew who could make a pilgrimage there on the great feasts.

A TEMPLE OF GOD

For Christians the central point in human history, the point toward which all preceding events were to reach fulfillment and from which all future events would unfold in integrated meaningfulness, is the Incarnation.

The Word was made flesh,
he lived among us,
and we saw his glory,
the glory that is his as the only
Son of the Father,
full of grace and truth (Jn 1:14).

God has spoken definitively His Word in the person of Jesus Christ. Everything that God had spoken in His actively creating Word is now fulfilled in Him:

At various times in the past and in various different ways, God spoke to our ancestors through the prophets; but in our own time, the last days, he has spoken to us through his Son, the Son that he has appointed to inherit everything and through whom he made everything there is. He is the radiant light of God's glory and the perfect copy of his nature, sustaining the universe by his powerful command; and now that he has destroyed the defilement of sin, he has gone to take his place in heaven at the right hand of divine Majesty (Heb 1:1-4).

Now God speaks His loving Word and "pitches His tent or tabernacle" and dwells among the newly chosen People of Israel. The active Word of God, was, from the beginning, as St. John points out in his prologue, creating new relationships with His People. Now He centers His presence in the "tent" of human flesh. The glory of God's divinity shone through the frailness and lowliness of His humanity. The glory or power of God in His Word radiated in the teachings and miracles of this man, Jesus. He touched people, looked upon them, loved them, spoke to them. His humanity is the point of encounter (as once in the desert the tabernacle was) through which the life of God could flow into the lives all who accepted Him. His sublime teachings were the *brightness* of God's own truth that turned human beings from the *darkness* of the ungodly and the sinful into children, born, not of flesh, but ''of God himself'' (Jn 1:13).

Jesus Christ, therefore, is the Word of faith in the sense that He perfectly and faithfully represents His Father in human communication of words and actions. Who sees Him, sees the Father (Jn 14:9). Jesus speaks God's complete presence to His People. Whether he heals a leper or claims absolute authority to forgive sins, Jesus is God communicating His Word in power. His actions, as Rudolf Bultmann says, are a speaking; whatever He says is action. [8]

But the power of Christianity consists in Christians believing and responding to this living Word made flesh, Jesus Christ, who died, rose from the dead and in the glory of the resurrection can now release God's Holy Spirit. The true, ongoing Christian New Age consciousness is made possible as we Christians live in the immanence of the risen Lord, Jesus Christ, who abides within us with His Father and the Holy Spirit. He makes it possible now for us to live a life that will never die. We need fear no one, for the very power of the Trinity dwells and operates from within us and through us in the world around us.

St. Paul grasped this ultimate climax and fulfillment of God's condescending love in communicating His Word to live with us, when he wrote:

> *Didn't you realize that you were God's temple and that the Spirit of God was living among you? If anybody should destroy the temple of God, God will destroy him, because the temple of God is sacred; and you are the temple (1 Cor 3:16-17).*

A LOGOS MYSTIC

To present a theology of Logos mysticism, I would like to summarize the thinking of St. Maximus the Confessor (+662), who is the most representative thinker in the early Church, especially among the Eastern Fathers, as regards Logos mysticism. For Maximus, as for St. John the Evangelist, the whole world is inter-related in its harmony according to the differentiated logoi, the created existences of individual creatures according to the mind of God. All things are created through the Logos through whom the creative will of the Father flows. St. Irenaeus in the 2nd century explains that the two hands of God bringing forth the universe are Jesus Christ and the Holy Spirit.

The logos in each being is the principle of existence which relates a given creature to God as its cause. It also denotes the created existence of a creature founded in God's will that it should have existence. It is the principle of a coming-to-be and implies a participation in God's being. These logoi are outside of time, existing in the mind of God and contained in the Logos, the Second Person of the Trinity, who is the first principle and final end of all creatures[9]

These logoi in the mind of God are not "inert models but the very creative power of God, realizing itself in the creature."[10]

CREATION AS A DYNAMIC PROCESS

Here we see a very dynamic vision of a world united in the mind of God, of a world of ideal logoi in process of being attained as the existential logoi in creatures move to completion under the power of the Logos, Jesus Christ and our human cooperation. Inanimate objects have to exist according to their God-given *logoi*. They have no free choice. An apple cannot be by free choice a peach tree.

But it is we human beings who have been placed by God as the center of this whole universe. We who share in God's likeness are given free will to become the consciousness and reflection to the rest of creation. But we also have the power, as the Israelites and as Adam and Eve had, to reject living according to our true logos in God's Logos. When we surrender to the Logos of God made flesh and gloriously risen and inserted into this material creation now in a new and amazing manner, we co-create our unique logos in God's Logos. But insofar as we are one in loving action of service to the world with the risen Lord, we also become co-creators — with God's glorified Word Jesus Christ and His Spirit — of the various logoi of all creatures in the almighty Logos of God.

Thus for St. Maximus and for ourselves as modern Christians, the truly human person is he/she who lives according to the individual logos that is always becoming in each moment as it becomes modeled on a conscious relationship in loving submission to the Logos living within that unique human being who brings forth the potencies to become the unique person God had always called by her/his name in His Logos.

CONTEMPLATING THE DIVINE LOGOS

St. Maximus used the term, *theoria physica*, to describe the contemplation — through the infusion of the Spirit's faith, hope and love — by the individual Christian of the inner logoi in the Logos of God's creative Spirit of love within all creation. The contemplative is able to move beyond the surface that presents itself to the senses, to arrive at an inner knowledge given by God that relates the given creature to the mind of God, to the Ultimate Source.

By knowing a thing in all its reality, the mystic intuitively sees its relationship to Jesus Christ. To quote Teilhard's phrase that perfectly summarizes the goal of Logos mysticism, the mystic begins to see "Jesus Christ shining diaphanously through the whole world." We must not think that God gives us a new gift called "infused contemplation." All things, as Irenaeus said, are held by God's two hands, Jesus Christ and the Holy Spirit. In the words of Gerard Manley Hopkins, S.J.: "These things, these things were here and but the beholder wanting."[11]

When we, through *praxis* or diligent inner attention, remove the impulsions toward self-love, and put on the mind of Christ as we live always in the Divine Logos (the virtuous life), we discover by God's infusion of deeper faith, hope and love what always has been the real world of God. We put aside the darkness and enter into a new Christian consciousness and are gifted to see reality from God's view through His Logos and Spirit of love.

Discovering the Logos in each event of each moment admits of many degrees of promptitude and surrender of oneself in obedience to the Divine Word. When we respond to our "inner self," our true person expands and becomes more open to further communications from God through His Logos. In all religions, especially in Christianity, after the initial encounter with God "outside," the believer turns within to encounter the divine Maker at the core that endowed the individual with a likeness to His Divine Logos. Our progression from an imperfect being to a more perfect one, from a lesser person to a more fully realized human being, consists in a gradual progression from the phenomenal world of choices, rooted in senses and passions, to be guided always by the determining motive of one's choice freely given as a conscious act of love to God.

We start with *eros* (what do I, as a god with a small *g*, get out of it?) and gradually we advance through unselfish love to *agape*, where the determining motive of our choice is love of God and neighbor, heedless of any reward to the self. Persons at different levels of personality and spiritual development express this inner core of being where their outflowing energy approximates closely the divine act of creation through the Divine Logos.

A man and woman, deeply in love, experience this divine creativity in their conjugal union when they leave selfish *eros* to find their own unique selves and to expand by giving without reserve to the other, to bring forth in that outflowing energy of life a new life, made in the image and likeness of God Himself. This creativity in union with the Logos reaches its highest union through *agape*, finding God in a sharing of His loving creation.

A mother working patiently to form her child, a Peace Corps worker in the heart of Africa, a religious or lay person teaching a class, all have experienced what it means to transcend the empirical, external *eros*-determinations in order to penetrate deep within themselves and, at the core of their being, to unite with the Divine Logos in the spark of divine creativity which enables them to give themselves in unselfish love for others.

FINDING THE LOGOS IN MATTER

One of the great dangers of modern life is that we have been allowing our senses to atrophy through our thermostated, controlled life. We find it difficult to hear the music in a child's voice, the rhythm of the traffic, the steady beat of our own heart. The touch of cool, cleansing water on a sweaty face has lost its restorative meaning for us. The taste of clean, freshly baked bread on hungry lips, the smell of the ozone in the air after a clearing rain, are lost experiences for most moderns. In a word, because we do not live intensely sensory experiences, we are no longer "open" to move from the material world to values of a more transcendental nature. We miss the unique logos that makes *this* rose so different from all roses because we fail to see it in God's Logos.

We have a great need today to re-educate our senses in order that they bring to consciousness sharp, vital, full sense experiences. This is the only way in which the material world can make contact with our interior selves, in which eventually the transcendent God can become truly the core of our immanent true selves as we discover the Logos working creatively in all of God's creation.

Can we not learn how to make contact with God's transcendent Logos present in all of His created, material world as we walk, step by step, down the hard concrete streets of our big cities? We could learn to see the different colors of God's world, in which He is vitally immersed and dynamically working, reflected mirror-like in the logos of each creature. The symbol of a drop of water in a Harlem gutter, able to mirror the whole world around it, God's world, but still more deeply able to symbolize as water, can lead us to the promise and hope of a newly cleansed life in God.

We have no other way to meet God, but by beginning with His created world. In the activities of our commonplace life, in the sense experiences overly familiar to us from a lifetime of routine, in every human being that we encounter through our senses, we have a contact point with God by discovering His Logos operating creatively as we work with Him in each material creature we touch.

INNER SILENCE

If we hope to discover the Logos working in all creatures, we in a way must learn also to withdraw from the material world and things in order to find God at the heart of the matter. To enter into the inner reality of things we must learn to leave the periphery, the noise, competition, all-absorbing anxieties and fears that militate against the silence and calm necessary for us to listen to God communicate Himself to us through His silent Logos, His single Word.

Besides the physical silence of our bodily parts as well as the psychic silencing of our emotions, imagination, memory, intellect and will, we need to descend into what Scripture calls "the heart." It is here that God speaks His Logos directly and immediately to us.

It is here that heart speaks to heart and we learn to surrender ourselves completely to let God's Word be done in our lives.

This is a state of highest expanded consciousness brought about by an increased infusion of faith, hope and love by the Holy Spirit. It is only the Holy Spirit who can teach us to understand what the single Word of God is saying to us. The Spirit reveals our unique and beautiful true self that we are to discover in our union with God's creative Logos. But it is also the Holy Spirit who brings forth His gifts and fruit in our relationships of loving service toward others.

Thomas Merton describes this inner silence and solitude:

> *It is here that you discover, act without motion, labor that is profound repose, vision in obscurity and beyond all desire, a fulfillment whose limits extend to infinity.* [12]

Such contemplative, silent listening will awaken a deeper sense of consciousness of the divine intelligence through God's Logos, who will bring us into an ever-expanding experience of a greater good and inner meaning and relationships in unity of all things in us and around us in their ultimate Ground of Being, in God Himself. Daily we open our consciousness to the divine energies, as we expect greater wisdom and guidance. Listening to the inner Logos of God's communicating presence, we will learn how to respond in harmony with God's leadings.

In awe, wonder and joyfulness before the Creator in union with His Divine Logos and Holy Spirit, we can listen to Him as He reveals through His Son and Spirit His secrets. His delicate promptings lead us toward new levels of transformation into a new creation (2 Cor 5:17). Such a prayer of the heart, with its constant fidelity to listen to God's Logos in life's events of each day, will bring us into a state of movement and tension. There is the tension of being in God with peace and tranquility, and the tension of not being in Him with its accompanying darkness and demonic forces that rise up from our past to haunt us into crippling fears and inner anxieties.

Yet God reveals His Logos as He speaks His creative Word in the darkness of all our human powers. We truly enter into the "cloud of unknowing" as the Logos leads us to relinquish our control over ourselves and over God and the world we have been creating according to our needs. This is that state of unconsciousness within us in which the untapped regions beneath the surface of existence are revealed by the Logos. When we reach this state that is devoid of all human words, thoughts, ideas and images, we are given by God's grace and mercy a kind of knowledge of God that our ordinary consciousness and efforts could never provide.

TRANSFORMING CONSCIOUSNESS

To the degree that the process of transformation takes place in us, so also will the liberating, illuminating, kindling spark of the infinite Light of the Logos shine more and more intensely until finally it becomes a basic part of our daily life. The center and meaning of life will now no longer be in persons or things outside of us, or, above all, in our own selfish beings, but only in the Divine Trinity. We are consciously now living "according to the image and likeness," that is Jesus Christ.

For such purified contemplatives the Spirit reveals the Father at every moment, unceasingly begetting the Son within them. The Son is never separated from the Father nor from the Spirit of love. The Word of God always directs us to the infinite Mind in their mutual Spirit of love. The contemplative lives in that abiding experience of the interpenetration of the trinitarian Persons, their energies shining through every part of his or her being.

The energizing light of God's loving presence is seen not only within the contemplative, but is seen bathing every creature outside in His glorious light. He is the Source of all life. He is energizing life. He gives life to everything that is. God's providence extends to every detail in the universe through the Logos, just as the light of the sun shines everywhere. If we do not see God's Logos as illuminating each creature in His all-pervasive, energizing presence, then we are blind and are not filled with His light. We are only in potential to become truly made according to the image and likeness of God that is Jesus Christ, the Logos made flesh.

The whole material world is the "locus" now for God's Logos to become present to us and to be served by ourselves in true, humble love. Although God is immovable, yet He is always seen by such a purified contemplative as movement. He fills all things, transcends all. He is immaterial, yet He pervades all matter.

TRANSFORMERS OF THE UNIVERSE

As we are purified of our own limited vision of reality and place ourselves by an ever-increasing infusion of faith, hope and love from the Spirit of Jesus Christ, God increasingly pours into us His Word. We live to let Him have His way, His Word, in our lives. "Be it done unto me according to thy Word" becomes for us our constant prayerful act of surrender as Mary, the Mother of the Word made flesh, continually said her *fiat* of surrender (Lk 1:38). We too are called by God to live according to His interior law that He wishes to write upon our hearts (Jr 31:33).

As contemplatives, we go out into the world of action with an interior knowledge because of our intimate relationship with God through his Logos and His Spirit. This penetrates every thought, word and deed as we seek to live out that Word interiorized and experienced through a constant listening within. Surrendering to God's uncreated energies, we begin to experience unsuspected areas of creativity. Our actions are now one with the movement of the indwelling triune community of perfect love. We place ourselves totally at the disposition of the divine energies. We gain such spiritual gifts as divine sight, divine hearing, the ability to read the hearts of other people. Above all, we develop love for the entire human race and for every creature alive and sustained by God's loving presence. This extends to a loving oneness with all animals, birds, plants and all of creation. We seek to serve and draw out the best hidden in each creature whom we meet.

This loving power is God's very own life, transforming the world into light and heat: the light that allows each human being to "see" God, loving us in each situation; and the heat to warm our hearts to adore the almighty, tender loving God as we open ourselves to love and serve one another. The love of God pours into us, allowing us to see the power of the Spirit of Jesus working in the lives of all human beings, regardless of culture or religion. We breathe more freely as we live on higher plateaus that stretch out into infinity. The walls and ghettos come crashing down that our fearful, anxious selves have constructed because we were living in darkness and ignorance and did not realize God was present in all things.

The world of matter is the place where God shines diaphanously forth. He is at the heart of matter. And matter is moving, by our prayerful contemplation of God working in His Logos, toward spirit. The world that is groaning in its limitations of matter is slowly emerging as a transfigured Heavenly Jerusalem (Rv 21:1-7).

4

Resurrection And A New Creation

One of the great modern prophets, who with blazing eyes pierces through the darkness and illusory values of this world and with rapier-pen calls us back to the inner, real world, is Alexander Solzhenitsyn. In his second volume of *The Gulag Archipelago*, he describes how he found the path to true inner freedom and enlightenment in a prison camp:

> *It was in my prison camp that for the first time I understood reality. It was there that I realized that the line between good and evil passes not between countries, not between political parties, not between classes, but down, straight down each separate individual human heart. . . . It was on rotting straw in my labor camp that I learned this and I thank you, prison, for teaching me this truth.* [1]

As we mentioned before, during the time of the great prophets (especially Isaiah, Jeremiah and Ezekiel), a new way of thinking about God and, therefore, a new sense of human individuation was given to the Jewish people. God now becomes for the chosen People personalized in His emotions, and in His actions of punishing, purifying and rearing His People.

— 75 —

Walther Eichrodt, the Old Testament scholar, describes this change:

Most remarkable . . . are the new form and forceful concentration of the relation with God, which had hitherto simply been described as the fear of God, and is now expressed in words like faith, love, thankfulness, and knowledge of God, which are filled with spiritual tension. [2]

This brought forth also a new consciousness on the part of the individual Jews. The individual person was emerging as someone who could with freedom choose to respond to God's personalized overtures. A breakthrough took place away from a collective obedience to God's extrinsic commands, to an obedience of authentic human freedom and responsibility. Again, Eichrodt describes this change: "The man to whom God's demand comes is recognized as a person, an I, who cannot be represented or replaced by any other."[3]

The Psalmist captures this axial, post-conventional consciousness as he cries out:

God, you are my God, I am seeking you,
my soul is thirsting for you,
my flesh is longing for you,
a land parched, weary and waterless;
I long to gaze on you in the
Sanctuary,
and to see your power and glory . . .
my soul clings close to you,
your right hand supports me
(Ps 63:1-2, 8).

Eric Voegelin offers us the prophet Jeremiah as the one who most clearly presents this immediacy of consciousness between the individual person and God:

*What is new in his extant work (Jeremiah) are the pieces of
spiritual autobiography, in which the problems of prophetic existence, the concentration of order in the man who speaks the word
of God, become articulate. The great motive that has animated
the prophetic criticism of conduct and commendation of the Vir-
tues had at last been traced to its source in the concern with the
order of personal existence under God. In Jeremiah the human
personality had broken the compactness of collective existence and
recognized itself as the authoritative source of order in society.* [4]

Thus with the prophetic tradition we see the ''axial''
breakthrough appearing, both in the lives of the great and authentic
prophets in Israel, and also among those Jews who accepted this
new consciousness of the individual before a personalized God.
We see the emergence of unique personhood and freedom among
individual persons of the Jewish religion. An autonomous *ego* now
stands before the almighty Yahweh and takes responsibility for
his/her human choices.

EMERGENCE
OF A CHRISTIAN CONSCIOUSNESS

Can we speak of Jesus Christ bringing a radical, new consciousness to the Jewish religion that, as He Himself insisted upon,
He came not to destroy but to fulfill (Mt 5:17)? Surely we cannot
deny that from the pages of the New Testament Jesus appears in
harmony with the prophets of old. He shows us a person most free,
especially about His own identity as a unique and free person,
acting with responsibility for all His actions that are ordered toward
doing always the will of the Heavenly Father.

Even though the Father is greater than He and He can do
nothing by Himself (Jn 5:30), yet He knows consciously at all times
that He is one with the Father (Jn 17:21). He knows clearly His
origin and His mission. ''. . . because I have come from heaven,

not to do my own will, but to do the will of the One who sent me" (Jn 7:16). He is to reveal the Father to the world. "To have seen me is to have seen the Father" (Jn 14:9).

All the attitudes of Jesus toward His fellow beings, His disciples, the Scribes and Pharisees, the sick whom He healed and His listeners who heard Him preach, all His words and actions were colored by a perfect freedom that grew out of His intimate relationship to the Father and His connected mission. He was aware of being God's Word and He knew that, as Word, He had to speak to the human race (Mt 11:29).

He was free from any spirit of Pharisaism. This He manifested in the freedom to move away from a slavish fulfillment of idolatrous forms and institutions without any individual surrender in the heart. This inner awareness of His personal relationship and union with the Heavenly Father colored His own conduct toward Jewish law and ordinances. He taught others that they should emphasize the inner consciousness rather than a magical performance of exterior signs to effect one's salvation.

But the key question is: did Jesus effect a breakthrough in a new "axial" consciousness that His disciples also experienced and passed on to others? John Cobb insists that Jesus transformed the Jewish teachings that He imparted to His followers to effect an emergence of a new way of viewing the ultimate reality:

My interest lies in the actual and effective emergence of a new structure of existence, and as a matter of historical fact, this occurred only by the total impact of Jesus' transformation of Jewish teachings combined with his resurrection appearances. [5]

From the New Testament we see how slowly during the lifetime of Jesus did His followers change from a lower level of understanding the "law and the prophets." It was only after His death and resurrection and through His appearances to His disciples that Jesus brought about through His Spirit a complete transformation and the beginning of the Christian community.

THE EMERGENCE OF A NEW AGE

The resurrection of Jesus is a new beginning which brings to an end the domination of historical time and space. And yet His resurrection happens within the orbit of earthly time and space, at least in its impact upon His disciples as shown by their new consciousness. They came to believe and to teach all over the Greek-speaking world in the Middle and Near East. They were even willing to lay down their lives for such beliefs.

They were vitally aware that God mysteriously had now entered into the history of humanity and from inside is setting about to destroy sin, corruption and death and is inaugurating a new form of existence called the *Kingdom of God.* This is done completely in Jesus, but gradually through His risen presence living in His members, who become one with Him, a new leaven in society to raise all humanity into a sharing of Jesus' new life.

A.M. Ramsey, the New Testament scholar, summarizes the impact of Jesus' resurrection which is "not merely a great event upon the plan of history, but an act that breaks into history with the powers of another world. It is akin to the creation in the beginning, and the Gospel is the good news that God is creating a new world."[6]

The resurrection of Christ is not only pivotal to the life and mission of Jesus; it is fundamental to God's actions throughout all human history. That is why St. Paul saw so clearly the centrality of Jesus' resurrection: ". . . if Christ has not been raised, you are still in your sins" (1 Cor 15:17). It is our Christian faith that Jesus died, but rose from the dead, and lives now in glory. He gives us through His Spirit a new consciousness that now He lives victoriously within each Christian. He intercedes for our human sins and restores new life to the Christian, but also He brings new life and fulfillment to all of God's creation.

SHARING IN HIS RESURRECTION

For us human beings to enter into the new creation brought about by Christ's resurrection and to live in the new consciousness that we have been redeemed through His death and resurrection, we need to be rooted in the historicity of the first community of Christian believers. How did they understand Christ's resurrection with its repercussions on their lives? The faith experience of the resurrection in the early Christian community as recorded in the New Testament must be grounded for our faith in the full meaning of the resurrection. Yet faith goes beyond historical criticism. The latter unfolds to us how Jesus' disciples came to believe.

But resurrection as an event that happened to the historical man, Jesus of Nazareth, cannot be verified by historical methods. Historical criticism can establish only that Jesus died and that the early disciples witnessed to His appearances and came to believe in Him risen. Faith, a gift from the Spirit of the risen Jesus, allows us in mystery to approach the resurrection as a statement about the death of Jesus whom the Heavenly Father raised up to glory and gave the power to bring new life and hope to all human beings.

The New Testament does not explain to our reasoning powers why the death of Jesus should have been necessary to new life. It merely states the necessity which is to be accepted and lived on faith. "Was it not ordained that the Christ should suffer and so enter into his glory?" (Lk 24:26). Faith invites us to enter into that faith-community and, thus united with those early believers of Christ, to die to selfishness so as to rise in living for others through God's Spirit of love.

ULTIMATE MEANINGFULNESS

Jesus has taken the sting out of death and given us meaningfulness beyond this temporal life that stretches into eternal life. He has "broken the power of death" (2 Tm 1:10). The Good News is that God so loved this world as to give us His only Son that we might believe in Him as the saving Lord and thus share in God's eternal life (Jn 3:16).

God's love is the ultimate meaningfulness beyond all man-made, rational explanations of what is really real. But this is a love that is self-emptying, *kenotic* in its outpouring of oneself in self-sacrifice for the other. No rational assault upon life's ultimate meaning can ever effect a surrender to the mystery of God's love for us, which covers itself with darkness when we probe with only our intellectual powers.

And, yet, to the broken ones of this world, who humbly cry out to God for the coming of His Love incarnated, Jesus Christ, into their lives, this mystery of love, that *death is resurrection*, is revealed. It becomes a living experience that cannot be taught and yet which grows into the fullness of reality as one enters into the *exodus-passover* experience of moving away from self-centeredness to God-centeredness.

GOD'S MIRACLE

Christianity is a religion that leads its faithful in a commitment to a person, Jesus Christ. Hinduism and Buddhism teach a way or path to enlightenment. Gautama Buddha is important for Buddhists because of his teachings. The historical details of his life are not important to them. Whether he rose from the dead or not is unimportant. What is important is how to reach his level of enlightenment and so attain the Buddha state of everlasting bliss.

To be a Christian is to put one's whole life in faith and loving obedience to the risen Jesus Christ, God-Man. He lived and was enlightened, but He also rose from the dead and now, according to the most essential element in Christian belief, He lives within us and shares with us through the release of His Holy Spirit His life everlasting.

It is by faith — given us as a gift from the Spirit of the risen Christ — that we *know* in a manner beyond all rational knowledge and wisdom that the historical Jesus of Nazareth is truly the incarnate Word of God, bringing us eternal life. Sometimes in prayer I am overwhelmed by the Good News of God's passionate love for all of us, His children — that the Trinity, God Father, Son and Holy Spirit, by what Teilhard calls "the game of the resurrection," wished through the risen Jesus immanently to give themselves to us individually at every moment of our lives in the similar self-emptying love of the historical Jesus who died out of love for us.

Something which has existed since the beginning,
that we have heard,
and we have seen with our own eyes;
that we have watched and touched with our hands:
the Word, who is life — this is our subject.
That life was made visible:
we saw it and we are giving our testimony,
telling you of the eternal life
which was with the Father and has
been made visible to us.
What we have seen and heard
we are telling you
so that you too may be in union with us,
as we are in union with the Father
and with his Son Jesus Christ.
We are writing this to you to make our own joy complete
(1 Jn 1:1-4).

RESURRECTION NOW

Yet for most of us Christians, the power of the resurrection has not always ushered us into a new age consciousness. This is due mainly to the fact that we wish to remain still on a level of subject-object consciousness and not to move into the mystery of an *I-Thou* relationship with God's immediate self-emptying community of love, the indwelling Trinity. Intellectually we give an assent that we call faith to the abstract truth that Jesus has risen from the dead.

We imagine in prayer that only Jesus' body died on the cross and the soul separated from the body that was placed in the tomb and returned to infuse the body and raise it to a new resurrectional life. Does this approach become a burning, gripping decision to discover Jesus risen at each moment of our lives that even now can be raised from the death of narcissism in the context of our present, broken world, suffocating from its bondage to "sin and death"? Are we Christians living lives in our contemporary society that demonstrate a higher level of consciousness, of oneness in love with God, all other human beings, with the entire universe, than those lived by humanists, atheists, Muslims, Hindus or Buddhists?

Does the reality of the historical Jesus who died and was raised by God unto glory give us a different Christ-consciousness from that induced by the latest techniques on mind-expansion which are marketed by innumerable seminars and workshops throughout our gullible land? If Christ *is* the resurrection, as He said (Jn 11:25), should this reality not be a daily experience for us Christians? Should this reality not make us completely different from non-Christians, especially in our loving service to build our universe into one of peace and justice for all human beings?

JESUS — THE CAUSE,
CENTER AND GOAL OF THE UNIVERSE

All God's creative power becomes completely concentrated in the person of the risen Jesus. St. Paul writes: "He was crucified through weakness, yet he lives by the power of God" (2 Cor 13:4). God fills His humanity with the fullness of His power and glory. "He was established Son of God in power by the resurrection of the dead" (Rm 1:4).

Because Jesus risen now possesses in His humanity the fullness of the Father's Spirit, we human beings can now receive of Jesus' Spirit. Jesus, by His resurrection, is now the "Prince of life" (Ac 3:15). He is now the cause, origin, center and goal of the entire world.

> *As he is the Beginning,*
> *he was first to be born from the dead,*
> *so that he should be first in every way,*
> *because God wanted all perfection*
> *to be found in him*
> *and all things to be reconciled*
> *through him and for him,*
> *everything in heaven and everything on earth,*
> *when he made peace*
> *by his death on the cross (Col 1:18-20).*

Jesus, the Pantocrator, the Almighty of the universe, makes it possible now for us to share in His resurrection. It means that we can be risen only insofar as we are united with the risen Lord and share in the one resurrection which is that of Jesus. The Father raises up only His Son. There is only His resurrection. We shall not be raised up apart from Jesus' single resurrection.

F.X. Durrwell in his pioneering work on the resurrection forcefully points out the singleness of our resurrection with that of Jesus:

This plan (God's saving plan) is put into execution with Christ's resurrection. The action whereby the body of the mortal Christ is transformed inaugurates the Father's action of justification, divine life comes to mortal man; the justice of God, which is a living and life-giving holiness, takes possession of him. It is the Father who raises up Christ (Rm 8:11; 1 Cor 6:14; 2 Cor 4:15; 13:4; Eph 1:19; Col 2:12) and who justifies us (Rm 3:26, 30; 8:30; Gal 3:8). It is in Christ and through the act of raising him up, that he justifies us. The resurrection of our Lord is the first of the Father's life-giving works in a new world, the first and only one, for all the others are accomplished in it: "He has quickened us together with Christ" (Eph 2:5).[7]

A CHOICE TO BE RISEN IN CHRIST

St. Paul, only at the end of his earthly life, evolved in the letters to the Ephesians and Colossians his teaching that even in this life we too can come to share in Christ's resurrection. In Baptism we Christians are buried with Christ and "by baptism, too, you have been raised up with him through your belief in the power of God who raised him from the dead" (Col 2:12). By taking away our sins and bringing us to life with Christ, God "raised us up with him and gave us a place with him in heaven, in Christ Jesus" (Ep 2:5-6).

This new life in Christ is already ours in Baptism and grows each time we "put on Christ" by dying to selfishness and rising to a new oneness with Him and in Him and with all other human beings. This new life that makes a "new creation in Christ" (2 Cor 5:17) is not yet in its fullness. Our bodily life, our total personhood, is in process of becoming more and more our true selves in Christ through our choices to live out our baptism at each moment in Christ. This life is hidden with Christ in God and will only appear with the manifestation of the fullness of Christ in His *parousia*

(His second coming in fullness). St. Paul's understanding of the resurrection had been earlier oriented to the future end of the world. But toward the end of Paul's earthly life, it became increasingly an experience in Christ that had already begun and is to increase as we cooperate to allow Him to operate in our lives.

RESURRECTION: A BECOMING EVENT NOW

God is now becoming our God and Jesus Christ is becoming *the* resurrection as we become living signs of the new creation by the love we allow to shine forth from our lives into the lives of others. We are daily destroying the temple with all its built-in idols as we allow Jesus risen to bring about the fulfillment of His words: "Destroy this sanctuary and in three days I will raise it up" (Jn 2:19).

Today is always becoming a new beginning, the first day of eternity, and is happening as we live death-resurrection in this present, *now* moment. We can interpret the beautiful words: ". . . as long as we love one another God will live in us and his love will be complete in us" (1 Jn 4:12) to mean: "As long as we love one another, Christ is more completely being risen in power and glory."

We will stretch out in hope for the fullness of Christ's coming in glory as we open up to the miracle of Christ's living, resurrectional presence in the concrete details of our daily lives to lead us from death to life, from non-reality to reality, from the darkness of mystery to the light of a new experience in His resurrection.[8]

A NEW TIME

As we make conscious connection with the risen Jesus in the context of our daily lives in each human situation, we discover (as the first Christians did) a new time that the risen Christ has made possible. St. Paul calls this "the time of salvation," and gives it the name of *kairos*. The historical time (in Greek, *chronos*), in which all people live, is for St. Paul the unredeemed past and present, our human history that is doomed to death and sin. The *kairos* interjects the horizontal time of our fleeting history to bring us into the new historical reality of Christ's resurrectional creation that allows us to live already in the end-time of the Kingdom of God.

The actual event of Jesus' resurrection was not witnessed by anyone on earth. Only those who were opened to the presence of Jesus as risen were able to "see" Him as risen. In addition, they were able to experience His glory and know that they were sharing already in it. Jesus could not be seen by those who did not believe in Him. He was no longer "observable" in human form as He was before His death. Then He was still one with a sinful world. There was something of the world's darkness in Him that allowed anyone to see Him with their physical eyes. He had laid aside His glory in becoming one with the sinful world. But now, "God raised this man Jesus to life and all of us are witnesses to that" (Ac 2:32).

The early followers of Jesus never yearned in a nostalgia to see, hear and touch Him as He was on this earth before His death. They had experienced an evolution in Jesus. He had progressed forward. Not only did the Father exult Him in glory and place Him at His right hand, but Jesus was now present to His disciples in a new time and a new presence. No longer is Jesus physically present to them as before in one limited place in Palestine. But the disciples of Jesus discovered that He was in His glorification now declared the living, eternal presence of God's love for each human being in all times. Jesus is now *Lord* of the universe and God of all. Doubting Thomas moves from historical knowledge to eschatological faith as he falls down to adore Jesus risen: "My Lord and my God!" (Jn 20:28).

A NEW PRESENCE

Jesus condescends to accommodate Himself to His disciples by appearing to them in apparitions, so that with a material body He was able to be seen, to speak, to eat, be touched by them and to carry the wounds of His passion. To meet Jesus as the new Creation, the disciples needed to make the step gradually from the historical Jesus to the risen Jesus.

Thus those eye-witnesses of the apparitions of the risen Jesus had a direct and personal experience of a "bodied" Jesus. It was because they did, that successive generations of Christian believers, including ourselves, could be brought into a "faithful" experience of the existing Jesus in glory. Mary Magdalene met the risen Jesus and mistook His physical form as that of the gardener. But she recognized Him in His word, "Mary," spoken to her. And Jesus said in effect to Mary: "Do not cling to me as you formerly knew and loved me . . . Go and find the brothers and there you will also discover me in the only way I wish to be present to you through faith" (cf. Jn 20:17).

Again Christ's message in His appearance to Thomas is: "You believe because you can see me. Happy are those who have not seen and yet believe" (Jn 20:29). St. Luke tells this truth of Jesus present to the Christian community in a new way, in the story of Jesus appearing to the two disciples on the road to Emmaus. The Evangelist wishes to teach the necessity of Christ's sufferings as a necessary part of His glorification. He also teaches that Christians can meet the presence of the risen Jesus in their personal sufferings and doubts and fears. Jesus explains the Old Testament writings of the prophets to show that the Messiah's glory is a part of His suffering servant role.[9]

But Luke also gives a deep teaching about the new presence of the risen Jesus to us who believe in Him. Although Jesus was physically present to the two disciples, nevertheless their eyes were kept from recognizing Him. They were still judging, not by faith within the context of the Word's presence and action to the community of God's people, but by the physical side of the Word. It was in the "breaking of the bread" that their eyes were opened to recognize Jesus present to them. Now we have a new presence in the risen Jesus that goes beyond His physical presence.

The Word of God is present and recognized as such, not by seeing Him, but by hearing the Christian community that gathers together through Jesus' Spirit and which speaks that Word in continuity with God's revelation in both the Old and New Covenants. There can be no full contact with the glorious, risen Jesus except in His Body, the Church, that in space and time now makes Him present to us.[10]

A NEW SPACE

Besides the space of meeting Jesus risen in the community of the Body of Christ (through the Word preached and obeyed within the Traditions of the extension of Christ, the Church, and in the sacraments, especially in the Eucharist), Jesus meets us as risen Lord in the space that lies within us. Scripture calls this space the "heart." It is there in the Spirit of faith, hope and love that we experience our true selves in being "in Christ Jesus." In the space of our hearts, in the deepest reaches of our consciousness, we encounter the risen Jesus in the spaceless space of His healing love.

We receive eternal life in the space of our oneness with the risen Lord. This new life in Christ has been ours in Baptism. It grows each time we put on Christ by an inner revolution (Ep 4:17). The work of the risen Jesus is to release within our hearts His Spirit. The Spirit reveals to us continually through the infusion of faith, hope and love that the Trinity of Father, Son and Holy Spirit truly dwells within us. "Didn't you realize that you were God's temple and that the Spirit of God was living among you? . . . The temple of God is sacred and you are that temple" (1 Cor 3:16-17).

THE INDWELLING SPIRIT

The Holy Spirit is raising us to higher levels of awareness of God's intimate presence to us. By pouring faith, hope and love into our consciousness, He makes it possible for us continually to be present to God at all times. The primary work of the risen Jesus is to release the Holy Spirit who teaches us all things we need to know about what Jesus did and taught during His earthly life (Jn 14:26). He will make us witnesses to the risen Lord (Jn 15:26-27).

Jesus risen is able in His Body, the Church, to share with us His full outpouring of the Spirit and thus to share with us even now as we live our lives in Him the one and only resurrection. Christ and we form one Body by the one Spirit of love (Ep 4:4). We and Christ are the recipients of the one vivifying action of the same Holy Spirit.

Now we too can share in the properties of God's Spirit as Jesus risen does. Jesus was put to death in the body, but "in the spirit he was raised to life" (1 P 3:18). "The Spirit of God has made his home in you" (Rm 8:9). As the body of the risen Jesus is spiritualized by the Spirit, so also, but not in the fullness yet, are our bodies holy and a temple of God in which resides the Holy Spirit (1 Cor 3:16; 6:19).

THE SPIRIT BRINGS US FREEDOM

The indwelling Spirit catches us up in an ongoing process of becoming God's children through His regeneration that allows us to be "born of the Spirit" (Jn 3:6). The light of the Spirit leads us out of all darkness and illusion. We are gradually enlightened by the light of His indwelling presence to know the truth that we are in Christ, even now, sharing a part of His risen Body. This same Spirit brings us into a sharing of Christ's resurrection by revealing to us that the same Jesus who died for love of us still loves us with that infinite love reached on the cross as He passed from death to resurrection. "For me he died," wrote Paul in a transforming knowledge given Him by the Spirit that dwelt within him (Gal 2:20).

As we yield to such a dynamic love of the present risen Jesus, who is progressively revealed to us through the Spirit and communicates Himself to us in His intimate self-giving, we experience a new freedom of being children of God, loved so immensely by God Himself. Fears and anxieties are shed as we experience new powers to love, to be "toward" God, ourselves, our neighbors, our cosmos. We experience a sharing in Christ's cosmic oneness with the entire, material universe, that brings about a eucharistic sharing as we touch and mould the matter of this universe into the Body of the risen Jesus.

Freed from sin by the light of the indwelling Spirit of Jesus risen, we no longer desire to live in darkness. "No one who has been begotten by God sins; because God's seed remains inside him, he cannot sin when he has been begotten by God" (1 Jn 3:9). As the Spirit constantly reveals to us from within our true identity as full, matured children of God, as children loved infinitely by a perfect Father through Jesus Christ who has died for us, we can live each moment in Him and with Him. We can learn to accept our true identity as fully matured children of God as Jesus was.

SENT TO BUILD COMMUNITY

The Holy Spirit brings us into a deep union with Jesus Christ so that His name is always on our lips and in our hearts. Our life becomes a *oneness* in Him as we seek to live each moment in the transcendence of the risen Jesus. This is the work of the Spirit (2 Cor 3:18).

Through the experience that is always ongoing of being one in Christ, living members of His very Body, the Spirit prompts us outward, not only to discover Christ in others, but to labor incessantly to bring Jesus forth in their lives. The Spirit is the builder of the Body of Christ. "There is one Body, one Spirit, just as you were all called into one and the same hope when you are called" (Ep 4:4).

As Jesus in His public life was anointed by the Spirit to go forth "to bring the good news to the poor, to proclaim liberty to captives and to the blind new sight, to set the downtrodden free, to proclaim the Lord's year of favor" (Lk 4:18; Is 61:1-2), so we are anointed by the same Spirit of Love to bring the good news to all men and women that they are uniquely beautiful as unique children of a loving Father.

Jesus extends His anointed work through His Spirit poured out into His members in order to take away sins, liberate human beings from all effects of sins and to bring about a new creation. This new creation will be the reconciliation of the entire world to the Father in fulfillment of His eternal plan in creating all things in and through His word.

"It was God who reconciled us to himself through Christ and gave us the work of handing on this reconciliation. . . . So we are ambassadors for Christ; it is as though God were appealing through us, and the appeal that we make in Christ's name is: be reconciled to God" (2 Cor 5:18-20).

CONFRONTING THE WORLD WITH THE SPIRIT

The risen Christ pours out His Spirit into our hearts in order that sin, the result of the world's darkness in us, be eradicated from us. But the Spirit within us drives us out into the world to confront the chaos, darkness and death that exist there. The life in the Spirit is to be a life of struggle against sin in whatever form it appears, both personal and social. The world cannot accept the Spirit since it neither sees nor recognizes Him (Jn 14:17). There is an aggressive hostility on the part of the world against the Spirit and the work of Christ to restore unity to the human race. The world will hate the disciples of Christ and persecute them (Jn 15:18-20).

But true Christians in the Spirit are not to run away from the world to wait for the "rapture." We are to be Christ's witnesses to His Gospel values by our lives lived in brotherly and sisterly love and unity. We are to be led by the Spirit of love to live non-violently. Even when persons unknowingly operate out of trans-cendent, self-forgetting love, as was demonstrated so powerfully in the life of Mahatma Gandhi, they are being guided by the Spirit. To sin is to assert selfishness over the Spirit of love that lives for loving service toward others and the universe.

One author well describes the working of the Spirit among those who serve others in true, self-emptying love, whether they do it knowingly or unknowingly:

> *Whoever rights wrongs, feeds the hungry, cares for the dispos-sessed not merely with enthusiasm but with dogged determina-tion, whoever is meek and poor of heart; whoever is sensitive towards the numerous little heartaches people suffer, is — know-ingly or unknowingly — an envoy of Christ. And whoever shares in Christ's mission, shares in the Fire of the Spirit.* [11]

THE SPIRIT BUILDS A NEW AGE

We may ask as we read today so much literature on New Age thinking: Is God in this? All truth is good because all truth is from God. Jesus said: "If you make my word your home you will indeed be my disciples, you will learn the truth and the truth will make you free" (Jn 8:31-32).

One respondent to my questionnaire mentioned in Chapter Three wrote these words to describe his view of the Spirit in the "New Age Movement":

The movement toward good nutrition, avoidance of killing drugs like tobacco and alcohol (and others) as guideposts for a good life seems to be good and from God. A small example: New Age people use crystals to heal . . . the rocks themselves are holy and sing their songs at frequencies which are inaudible to human beings. Their songs are a kind of residual vibration from the Big Bang — a kind of song about the Power of God. There is more healing and more peace around us and within us in our everyday existence than there is disease, injury and unresolved anger and fear within us. What we hear called "the spiritual world" — the world of thoughts, prayers and intentions, is being revealed through the discoveries of various scientific disciplines as new aspects of physical reality.

It seems to me that the physical world and the spiritual world were, are and always will be One. This is an insight which modern science, prayerful people, and New Age people can share with each other and the entire world. . . . On a practical level: God listens to Hail Marys, to "oms," and to the terrible racket all our blood vessels make as they contain all our blood within their walls the whole of our lives. And He listens to the winding music of DNA double helixes, and to the wild buzzing of innumerable orbiting electrons in even one drop of water. The symphony of all these vibrations and movements and prayers is called "One" and "Love."

The true Christian is always a humble pilgrim, always searching deeper into a reality that is permeated by the triune presence of Father, Son and Holy Spirit. God is a fullness, an inexhaustible source of love that seeks continuously to share His very being with us human beings. But He seeks to reveal Himself as a community of self-emptying, individuated persons, as a Trinity, to those who move beyond the type of religion which allows us to fashion God and the world and others after our own image.

But to the little ones of this earth, the poor of spirit and clean of heart, the unseen God reveals through His Holy Spirit how simple bread and wine can open us up to the living Bread of life, Jesus Christ, true God and true man. Through such eucharistic encounters such little ones move into the world and find the presence of the risen Jesus, not only in bread and wine, but in the little pebble, the smile of a child, the sparkle in the eyes of a wise old man. The whole world is a part of the eternal Liturgy that the Lamb of God is offering to the Heavenly Father.

The heart of all reality is Eucharist: receiving God's great love for each of us individually in His Son incarnated, Jesus Christ, through the illumination of the Holy Spirit, who empowers us to return that love in self-surrendering service to each person we meet.

CHRIST IS MY NEIGHBOR

When God's self-emptying, *kenotic* love overcomes us through the Holy Spirit of the indwelling risen Jesus, we realize that everyone is our neighbor and we are God's beautiful children. But it is more than this. Transformed by God's alluring presence as burning, fiery love immanently dwelling within us, we are empowered by this love, the Holy Spirit, to be self-emptying love to our neighbor.

We not only love all people and the entire universe with God's unconditional love, but we are really loving God, who is immanently present in all created beings. Then we will understand (because we will have lived it out) Jesus' discourse about the final judgment: "For I was hungry and you gave me food. . ." (Mt 25:34-40).

To look on the face of a son or daughter of God is to see a holy face. Our neighbors all over the world, of all colors, cultures and creeds may not realize how beautiful they are in God's passionate love for them individually. In their loneliness, fears and anxieties they may be unaware of God's emptying love from within them.

But you and I are called by faith to go beyond the externals. God's Spirit allows us to enter by loving service into the core of our neighbor's being where God abides as the compassionate and co-suffering community of *I-Thou* in the Trinity. There we touch God and neighbor, a unity in diversity, God, one with His suffering human child.

Our neighbor is the face of Christ Himself. It may be defaced. Yet we are called to the great dignity of restoring (with God's involving, uncreated energies of love) the fullness of that beauty. Jesus, the suffering servant of God, lives in us, loves in us and wishes to serve his broken brothers and sisters through us. He is risen, but He wishes to work through our weaknesses to raise this world into the Garden of Eden God had intended it to be when He decreed to create all things in, through, and for His Word.

By God's presence as self-emptying love in Jesus Christ, we are empowered to beget God's actualized presence in the neighbor whom we serve, and in the world we are called by God to co-create with Him. By dying to ourselves and rising to a new consciousness of oneness with the risen Jesus living within us, we can live for all others. We can find our true selves by losing our lives and finding them in the oneness in love with the others whom we lovingly serve.

THRILLING THE HEART OF THE FATHER

Loving, humble service to our brothers and sisters and a faithful, energetic stewardship over the material world to create a better world for all is the sign that Jesus is Lord. It is sign that we are privileged even now to share in His resurrected life by becoming the focus of God's creative Word in the cosmos. He is revealing a Father who also is a suffering servant, as His Image was during His life on earth.

This loving Father brings us and all of creation into an on-going oneness with Jesus Christ, who is one with God and is still the otherness in His oneness with us and all of material creation. The resurrectional presence of Christ living and working through us in a new age consciousness makes it possible to believe that all our actions will last forever and continuously thrill the heart of God, the Lover of mankind.

5

The Christic Universe

In one of his assemblage sculpture
pieces entitled "The Crucifix," Albert Ceen, an American artist
now residing in Rome, has made the body of Christ on the cross out
of cast-off junk. The face of Christ is fashioned out of a bicycle
chain; monkey wrenches inserted into one another form the stark
outline of Christ's arms and hands. A stovegate forms His halo.
Parts of an automobile transmission form His chest, legs and feet,
while a gnarled-up chain forms the loin cloth.

The artist found Christ's body in the junk. The initial reaction
of most viewers is one of shock, not only at the almost macabre
effect of neo-realism that the artist captured in the sufferings of
Christ, suggested by the bare bone structure, but at the mere fact
that he should have used such "unspiritual" objects to fashion the
sacred, suffering body of Christ.

But after a while, the spectator's consciousness enters into the
sculptor's vision, and one begins to see what he saw. This message
is fundamentally what Pierre Teilhard de Chardin was trying to
teach. With us Teilhard, the Jesuit scientist-philosopher-mystic,
asks:

"Will the material world remain ever closed to modern human beings in their attempts to find God? Will we yield ourselves to

the material world, whose many mysteries we do not understand, as though it were uncontrollable, and hence incomprehensible to the human mind? Or will we merely abandon the material world and any possibility of ever rising through it to find God in the very heart of matter?''

We, too, can ask the question that Teilhard asked in 1927 when he wrote his most complete synthesis of his spiritual vision, *The Divine Milieu*:

''Is the Christ of the Gospels, imagined and loved within the dimensions of a Mediterranean world, capable of still embracing and still forming the center of our prodigiously expanded universe? Is the world not in the process of becoming more vast, more close, more dazzling than Jehovah? Will it not burst our religion asunder? Eclipse our God?''[1]

NEED FOR A CENTER

To say that most modern persons are confused and without a center or ground for their being is to repeat cliches already over-worked in the literature of existentialism. Still we see our world exploding and expanding with a frightening degree of complexity and multiplicity. We seem to be helpless atoms, bombarded by myriads of material creations, all threatening to destroy our oneness-in-being.

Mircea Eliade, in his work, *The Sacred and the Profane*, has shown that primitive man instinctively sought to center, and thus unify, the indeterminate, amorphous mass of his daily experience. He found this center within himself toward which his total person could be ordered as toward the ground of his real self. He drove a stake into the earth, thus symbolizing the pinning of a snake's head — a sign of chaos and unreality — to the ground.

This spot on earth gave him a second center, and upon it he built his home. Next, he joined his clansmen in a hunt, and where the prey was killed he built his temple, the center of his social community. He chose a mountain top as the center of his cosmos, and there he encountered the Supreme Reality of his world.

Christians do not need to search for the center of their lives, their homes, their social community and their cosmos. That center became a reality when the sacred intersected with the profane in the person of Jesus Christ. God, the Supreme Reality, became centered in a human body. "The Word became man and lived among us" (Jn 1:14).

Human beings now had a center toward which they could direct their whole life. "All things came into being through him and without him there came to be not one thing that has come to be" (Jn 1:3). All things have their true reality when grounded in Christ. He is the Alpha and the Omega (Rv 1:8) of all created beings and "in him we live and move and have our being" (Ac 17:28).

THE CHRISTIAN VISION

This is the vision of Christians of all times. The sacred in the person of Jesus Christ is the center now of the profane, giving it its order, its unity, its fullest reality. Through the profane element of His human body, Jesus Christ has inserted Himself into our lives and into our cosmos. Because that human body died and was raised to a new and glorious life in the resurrection, that sacred center is still inserted into the profane of our lives and of our cosmos. He will never cease being the center of all reality.

Still, Christians not only believe that all reality comes under His dominion, but also hold by deepest faith that Jesus Christ, through and in His resurrected body, is working to accomplish the fulfillment of all creatures. By an interior force of attraction called love, He draws to Himself human beings, capable of recognizing and acknowledging Him as their center of true being. Christian faith brings with it the awesome possibility and obligation of building within ourselves a sacred temple, of relating ourselves to a center who is the risen Christ, living within us. ''Do you not know that you are God's temple and that God's Spirit dwells in you?'' (1 Cor 3:16)

From within us, Christ permeates and leavens the profane world in order to make ''all things in Christ,'' as St. Paul so forcefully puts it (Col 3:11; Ep 4:6; 1 Cor 15:28). It is Christ who fills all things and in whom everything is held together (cf. Col 1:17).

ENCOUNTERING GOD MORE IMMEDIATELY

For those who believe in a God who transcends this sense world, or for the confused and frustrated who would like to believe in something or someone bigger or more enduring than this fleeting pleasure or that past joy, there is a desire or an unexpressed hope to approach such a Transcendent Being *immediately*. Rituals and rites, symbols and priests have apparently lost most of their usefulness for the modern generation.

Yet many Christians, who unfortunately see their religion as all too often a flight from the material world, vainly try to reconcile their strong attraction to the world with a basic distrust of it. Christians today are faced with a religious crisis that ultimately centers on the person of Jesus Christ. Does the Christ traditionally presented to them in religion classes and Sunday sermons have relevance for them, absorbed as they are in fashioning a new and exciting world? How can they find Him, the Source of all life, in this complex, ever-changing world of today?

The ''other-worldly'' Christians who feel they must flee from the ''evil'' world will also deny (contrary to basic Christianity from all centuries) that God can be found in the world He created and that His Kingdom consists in the transfiguration of His world into a "new creation," a "Heavenly Jerusalem." Such Christians will repress their taste for God's material world and focus their interest on purely religious objects. They will seek to rule out of their lives as many "worldly" objects as possible.

Another dangerous temptation for Christians today is the opposite reaction, namely, to completely immerse oneself in this world as the total and only milieu for human existence. Such a belief includes an extreme optimism that trusts solely in human resourcefulness to create a "lasting city" on this earth. The premise of such utopian "secularism" is that all religions, including Christianity, are irrelevant for the only "world" there is.

Perhaps the majority of Christians are unable to choose between an "otherworldly" rejection of the world, and a total immersion with the things of this earth. They want so much to be "religious," with an implicit rejection of the things of this world. But again they wish to be citizens of this world with all its richness and allurements.

But there is another, more valid Christian view toward our world and the means to encounter God in matter.

DISCOVERING GOD IN MATTER

Incarnational theologians, such as Maurice Blondel, Henri de Lubac, Hans Urs von Balthasar, Karl Rahner and Pierre Teilhard de Chardin stress the unity between God and His world, between the supernatural and the natural, between grace and nature. These thinkers start with an optimistic vision of God's dominion over His created world and a trust that He could and would attain the end which He intended in creating this world. Grounded in the writings of the early Fathers of the Church, they insist that God is to be encountered precisely in and through the world, the very world cursed by God (Gn 3:17-18).

God so loved this world as to give His only begotten Son, who came to establish His kingdom on this earth. This kingdom, wherein Christ becomes present to His creatures, is hidden within the material world, like a leaven in a mass of dough. Faith shows us Christ immanently working to transform and complete God's creation. Instead of fleeing from the material world, we are to encounter Christ in that "secular" world.

All created beings exist through Christ and are sustained in their being by His activities. He is the Logos, the image according to which, not only we human beings, but all creation are fashioned. Through Him each creature will attain its completion. "All things came into being through him, and without him, there came to be not one thing that has come to be" (Jn 1:3). ". . . in him were created all creatures in the heavens and on the earth. . . . All have been created through him and for him" (Col 1:16-17).

A PAULINE VISION

In Chapter Three we have seen how St. John highlights Jesus Christ as the Logos. In the writings of St. Paul and the Greek Fathers of the first seven centuries who followed his view of the Cosmic Christ, Christ is presented as immersed in and energizing the created, material world. In Paul's captivity letters, especially to the Colossians and Ephesians, Christ is presented as the center of unity for all that has been created.

Paul strives to define more precisely Christ's relationship, not only to individual human beings, but also to the whole cosmos. Christ appears as the center of unity, drawing all things back to their origins. Since the world was created for Christ (Col 1:6), it must be recapitulated or reestablished in and through Him under whose power all creatures must one day be reunited.

RECAPITULATION IN CHRIST

St. Paul uses the word *anakephaloioomai* (Ep 1:9-10) to describe Christ's role assigned in the decree of His Heavenly Father, namely, that when the fullness of time would arrive, God would gather all creation, both in heaven and on earth, under one head, Christ. H. Schlier finds a great variety of possible meanings for this term as it is used in Scripture, but *reestablish* seems to be the best translation.[2]

We can accept this term to mean that Christ will restore the world's lost unity under His own headship in a unity of love. Christ at the time of His death and resurrection, in microcosm as it were, reestablished or reconciled humanity in Himself by destroying sin, death and the distorted element in the flesh. In the second coming He will also reestablish all things, "raising up the flesh of the whole of mankind," by spiritualizing it. He will bring all things completely under His dominion by bestowing the fullness of His divine life upon His human brothers and sisters for all eternity.

Yet, in a very true sense, this reestablishing of divine life in the individual person need not wait for the *parousia* or second coming. The process has already begun in human beings through Baptism and the increase of faith. Again, we see Christ's own bodily death and resurrection as the perfect type of our own individual dying to the "'carnal'" elements in order that we might be reestablished by Christ's grace into the new creation in Him (2 Cor 5:17-20).

J. Huby, the Pauline scholar, synthesizes how Christ will gather up all things to give them their fullest meaning in Himself:

> *In Him all has been created as in a supreme center of unity, harmony, and cohesion, which gives to the world its sense, its value, and therefore its reality. Or, to use another metaphor, He is the focus, the "meeting point" as Lightfoot puts it, where all the fibres and generative energies of the universe are organized and*

gathered together. Were someone to see the whole universe, past, present and future, in a single instantaneous glimpse, he would see all beings ontologically suspended from Christ, and completely unintelligible apart from Him. [3]

REDEMPTION OF THE CREATED WORLD

The Semitic mind, and Paul follows the same thinking, conceived human beings and the material world in which we live as a unit, a community of interrelated beings on march in a spiral process to their completion. In the final attainment of the end toward which all creation was moving, divine revelation gave to St. Paul an understanding of the total redemption of the universe which would be completed in the *parousia.*

Paul shows us, not only that the universe is an instrumental means of our redemption, but also that every created being itself is to be an object of Christ's redemptive power. This physical universe is in travail to be born to a new life. It is our Christian hope that God does not create for death, annihilation, or frustration, but rather to perfect His creatures into the fullness of their participated being.

Thus, our hope assures us that both our God-created soul and our God-created body will be touched by the glorious resurrected life of the Savior and be brought to the fulfillment God had planned in His original creation. But if our material body will be transformed and not destroyed, Paul assures us, this will also apply to the total cosmos. The whole created order will be brought into the glorification of the full Body of Christ. Thus Christ, as Head of the created cosmos, can bring it back, complete and full, to its Maker and Final End (1 Cor 15:28).

A PATRISTIC VISION

The early Eastern Fathers theologized out of Scripture and not in the abstract. They defended the Christian faith against the encroachments of various heretical teachings such as Gnosticism, Arianism, Monophysitism and Nestorianism. Most of these early theologians kept alive the vision of the cosmic Christ as taught by St. Paul and St. John. This was the theme of my first published work, *The Cosmic Christ: From Paul to Teilhard.*[4] I tried to show that the Pauline and Johannine incarnational theology was kept alive up to the 7th century through such writers as Irenaeus, Origen, Clement of Alexandria, Athanasius, Gregory of Nyssa, Gregory Nazianzus, Cyril of Alexandria and, above all, Maximus the Confessor.

We cannot expect, with the Fathers' level of scientific knowledge, that they would present us with a detailed vision of interrelationships of all material creatures and their mutual dependence. However, it is their total, unified vision of faith that is most enriching for us to build our own vision of the cosmic Christ. Such a vision will be enriched with our present knowledge of nuclear physics and the development of Christian theology through more advanced studies in Scripture, linguistics, archaeology and liturgy. By viewing human beings in relation to God, to fellow human beings and to the rest of the created world from the fourth dimension of God's finality, the Eastern Fathers were able to avoid the dichotomy that in the West was mainly responsible in theological thought for the diminishment of the cosmic dimension of Christ's activities in our present world.

Rather than an antithesis between *nature* and *supernature*, they opposed *natural* and *unnatural*. *Nature* was not only the embryonic seed, but the fulfillment in all the creature's final fruition. Human nature was always destined — not only by God's finality in creating human beings, but also in God's loving activity to accomplish His plan — to make human beings divinized children of God, sharing in His very own nature (2 P 1:4). We, as total entities of body, soul and spirit levels, were meant to move in a continuous process of loving activities in the cosmos to a more conscious relationship to God and to the world.

The Greek Fathers stressed a harmonious synergism of mutual cooperation that preserved the full gratuity of salvation and yet required human beings to overcome self-centeredness by virtuous living, especially by love. Such love is the bond of unity and harmony among human beings that does most to restore their dominance and proper stewardship over the rest of creation. These Fathers stressed that through His incarnation, Jesus Christ was also in the midst of the material world exerting His victorious power to bring the whole created order into its fullness through the instrumentality of other human beings, motivated by reciprocal love toward Him.

The Church was seen as the sign wherein the created cosmos entered into a transfiguration, and through its instrumentality the resurrectional life of Jesus Christ was extended to the cosmos. Retaining its own individuality, each creature was able to be assumed into a new transcendent relation with God as its end. The material world, through the Church, meets the spirit. Retaining its materiality, it still participates in a new existence of spirituality. The *eschaton* (the final goal), through the Church, has been realized in the *now*, but *not yet* fully.

The resurrection of Christ is applied to the transformation of the world into ''God in all'' to the degree that the baptized in Christ rise from a self-centered life to put on a new life in Him. The rest of the world waits for human beings to stretch out in a yearning (*epectasis*) that will be climaxed only in the *parousia* when Jesus Christ shall come to render explicit what was always implicit, to reveal what was hidden, to fructify the powers in creation which were lying there in potency.

The work of the Eastern Fathers of the first seven centuries was well done. The Church needs to recover these insights and develop them further into a Christian New Age consciousness. These early Christian Fathers can lead us to the "within" of matter. There in great humility and reverence for God's "numinous," *within* transcendence, they show us, through their teachings on God's uncreated energies of love, how to discover the immanent presence of God, who is in the process of co-creating with us the world of diversity into unity through love.

A NEW WORLD

Yet their teachings, based on God's revelation through Scripture and their own mystical experience, are seemingly inadequate to convince us moderns. They did not possess the knowledge we do today through our science that reveals to us our universe as one of gigantic proportions, of staggering energies and masses and of chaotic upheavals with great potentiality for destruction as well as creativity.

Their world view had all things created directly by God. Their theology gave a simple picture of the purpose and direction of the cosmos. Modern scientific discoveries unfold to us a world of tremendous energies on all macrocosmic and microcosmic levels. The apparent "faith" view of the early Fathers does not help us to cope with the great paradox of the co-existence of apparent order and purpose with chaos and purposelessness. We struggle with order and disorder, with necessity and change, with good and evil as opposites, in a world that is expanding through an exploding process of continued evolution.

Can we not see what difficulties our separation of two ways of knowing has brought to our modern world? Scientists give us a knowledge of the universe in all its complexities as they probe back in time to the origin of the universe in the "big bang." They split the atom and tell us of the minute complexity of the subatomic particles. Yet scientists, in their discovered world of chance, randomness and chaos, cannot tell us where the world process is going and whether a synthesis of order and harmony will ever result at the end of the struggle.

I would like to present a "new age" consciousness of our relationships to the cosmos by highlighting some of the key intuitions found in the writings of Teilhard de Chardin. He insisted that his views were not really new but a development out of the writings of St. John, St. Paul and the Greek Fathers. His rich insights can help us to love the universe of matter and find God through Christ, immanently present in each atom and directing all, with our human, free cooperation in love into greater complexities of diversity in unity through creative action.

AN EVOLVING UNIVERSE

Teilhard's starting point is the evolutionary process which he considers a proven fact and not merely a hypothesis or theory. He projects this process into the future with his theory of the ever-converging universe, moving with greater affinity to Spirit. Into this scientific view he injects his Christian faith based on revelation, especially as given to us in the inspired writings of St. John and St. Paul.

Science and religious faith comprise two different sources of knowledge, but do not contradict each other. They both lead to the same Center. Teilhard brings the evolutionary process into these two types of knowledge: one scientific and the other mystical, intuitive and experiential. The Oxford scholar of Eastern religions, R.C. Zaehner, describes Teilhard as "a prophet and a mystic . . . one of the greatest mystics of all time."[5]

Cardinal Henri de Lubac, who knew Teilhard intimately, cautions us in reading Teilhard to keep ever in mind this very legitimate fount of true knowledge, the mystical:

Pere Teilhard was a mystical thinker, but he was even more truly a mystic. He was one of those "souls that have a vision". . . . If rationally analyzed, there is always, we must recognize, an element of ambiguity in the language of the mystics. This is not because it is always imprecise, but because what is precisely expressed is not what we expected. . . . The mystical paradox — which is not theological in exactitude, nor a verging on the poetic — expresses the dialectic of an interior world which is foreign to pure intellect. What is more, it is seldom that true mystics can avoid meeting, at the outset, with an opposition. . . . This is because with the true mystics, we feel we are getting out of our depth; because they seem to jeopardize more of the things we customarily accept; and because at the same time, we feel obliged to take them more seriously. [6]

Teilhard was able through his expertise in science and in religious thought to take the spiritual and material poles of his faith and see in them the dynamic undercurrent of the whole evolutionary process. One of his greatest contributions to modern religious thinking is his conception of reality as composed of both spirit and matter. With modern physicists, he would maintain that matter could no longer be seen as static, inert and dead. We were called to discover God as part of the "withinness" inside of all matter. In his classic, *The Phenomenon of Man*, Teilhard describes the *within* and the *without* in all of matter:

It is impossible to deny that, deep within ourselves, an 'interior' appears at the heart of beings, as it were seen through a rent. This is enough to ensure that, in one degree or another, this 'interior' should obtrude itself as existing everywhere in nature from all time. Since the stuff of the universe has an inner aspect as one point of itself, there is necessarily a double aspect to its structure, that is to say, in every region of space and time — in the same way, for instance, as it is granular: coextensive with their With-*out, there is a* Within *to things.*

The consequent picture of the world daunts our imagination but it is in fact the only one acceptable to our reason. Taken at its lowest point. . . primitive matter is something more than the particulate swarming so marvelously analyzed by modern physics. Beneath this mechanical layer we must think of a 'biological' layer that is attenuated to the uttermost, but yet is absolutely necessary to explains the cosmos in succeeding ages. The within, consciousness *and then* spontaneity — *three expressions for the same thing. . . .*[7]

A LOVE OF THE UNIVERSE

Certainly the Christian significance of the universe is no merely marginal theme for Teilhard. It lies at the very heart of his intellectual and spiritual quest. He notes in his very first essay of the war years (WW I):

I write these lines to express an impassioned vision of the earth, and in an attempt to find a solution for the doubts that beset my action — because I love the universe, its energies, its secrets, and its hopes, and because at the same time I am dedicated to God, the only Origin, the only Issue, the only Term. I wish these pages to radiate my love of matter and of life, and to harmonize that love, if possible, with the unique adoration of the only absolute and definitive Divinity.[8]

Teilhard felt himself motivated by love of God, but also by a love for the universe. The dynamic interplay of these two loves would function as a catalyst for his entire life's work. He linked his consideration of the universe with his theological reflections on human beings, just as he tied these latter reflections to his Christological thought.

By *universe* Teilhard means the evolutionary thrust of the totality of creation, including human beings. The latter are at the forefront of the process, but also profoundly rooted in its whole. He, as an internationally famous paleontologist, saw the roots of our humanness plunging back and down into the unfathomable past.

''It is through the world that God envelops us, penetrates us, and creates us . . . our spirit is bound by all kinds of fibres and roots to the *material matrix* and is dependent upon it for its life.''[9]

We, too, today can confess with Teilhard that, if we are to treat of ourselves as human beings with meaningful goals, we must also treat of ourselves *and* the universe. No part of theological reflection — whether we are probing our creation, fall, redemption or glorification in Christ — can be fully developed without probing our cosmological roots and mutual goals. Christ saves human beings *and* the universe.

We are a most vital, even the conscious reflection and self-directing, part of the process of the entire universe's development into greater diversity in unity through loving conscious creativity. Our cosmos is no longer able to be conceived in static terms, but as a process of development. It is a *becoming* universe and we are also a part of *becoming* vitally ''human'' in that same evolutive process.

> *In the space of two or three centuries, and under the converging influence of a number of factors . . . it has become impossible to present the universe to us in the form of an established harmony: we now see unmistakably that it is a system in movement. It is no longer an* order, *but a* process. *No longer a cosmos but a* cosmogenesis.[10]

In *The Phenomenon of Man* Teilhard painstakingly traces this cosmogenesis from the first created proton to atoms, molecules, minerals, to embrace a *biogenesis* of plant and animal life until human life: the *noogenesis* of the development of intellectual, human life. This path includes the pre-human pithecanthropus and sinanthropus, on up to *homo sapiens* by way of the neanderthaloids. Human man and woman stand above all other creatures of the universe and cry out: ''We alone know and we know that we know!'' Only we, among all material creatures of God, possess the unquenchable longing for eternal life. We alone can turn within ourselves and reflect on the purpose of our being and our relations to all other beings and to the Ultimate Source of all being. We can penetrate the mystery of life, discover the purpose behind this movement of evolving multiplicity and even foster or hinder the process.

Matter has always been moving to higher forms of greater complexity in molecular structure with a proportionate development in consciousness. [11] With the advent of human beings possessing the power of reflection, a living being becomes the center of personalization. Even this personalization evolves from a self-centered person, intent on self-preservation, to a being going out through communication and a conscious act of love for ''another self.'' The entire process of ''hominization'' of human beings unites humanity into a unity of multiple complexity and differentiation.

CHRISTOGENESIS

We human beings, through our free will, have the power to move the universe toward its final and complete goal which Teilhard terms *christogenesis*. Such an evolution is not a predetermined process that both denies God's gratuitous gifts of grace and our free will cooperation. We can abort or at least push back this progress that is meant to move forward and upward. We can freely cooperate with the ''withinness'' of God as Spirit of love inside of matter, inside ourselves, inside the entire universe. Without such cooperation all human achievements and so-called progress are to be reckoned meaningless.

Teilhard links up the full purpose of the Incarnation with the completion of the universe in its ultimate goal and purpose:

> *If the world is convergent and if Christ occupies its center, then the Christogenesis of St. Paul and St. John is nothing else and nothing less than the extension, both awaited and unhoped for, of that noogenesis in which we experience the culmination of cosmogenesis. Christ invests himself organically with the very majesty of his creation.* [12]

THE OMEGA POINT

Before Teilhard can identify the process of evolution as culminating in Jesus Christ, he describes what he calls the *Omega Point*. He sees the process moving through different layers of consciousness, measured by greater unity in diversity through creative love, much as in the form of a cone. The tip or point of the cone Teilhard calls *Omega*, which is the name in the Greek alphabet given to the last letter, hence meaning the final goal or completed purpose of creation. This is the goal toward which evolution is moving, the point of convergence of all inferior lines which meet in it.

Before he identifies this Omega Point with Christ, Teilhard describes it in greater detail. The ultimate point, drawing not only all human beings, but all the universe through reflective human beings as the universe's fulfillment, manifests three characteristics:

1) It must be of an objective nature; it cannot exist merely in the human imagination. Creation and the evolutionary process must have a concrete end toward which they are moving.

2) It must have the power in itself to draw, by its own activity, all creatures into a unity to their full consummation. In order to draw intellectual beings, this point of attraction must also

be an intellectual being, a person. This person must do this through his own power, goodness and ultimately, through the act of love by which a person draws another into the highest union of self-communication.

3) It must be able to move the entire universe to its united perfection without any fear of regression, destruction or total frustration. [13]

JESUS CHRIST IS THE OMEGA POINT

When Teilhard strives to clarify and "incarnate" the Omega Point, he is accused of having left science and moved into the orbit of his Christian faith. Through an extrapolation he finds himself at a point that his Christian faith could alone bring him. Beyond scientific research, Teilhard argues that the process of evolution must converge upon a real, existing point of unity. As we have seen, such a person must exist and yet transcend all other created beings. This person must be immanently inside the process and yet be also outside of it. This person must not be created by the resulting convergence of humanity, but must be the moving force that converges and draws the diversity of human persons into a real unity around this center of attraction. This person has to be spiritual since he attracts other spiritual beings as their fulfillment. He must be eternal and transcendent, the fullness of being, never adding to his being, but possessing all perfections desired by mankind in its ever-growing thirst for more being, for a richer and more intense life.

This person, finally, must be immanent. Only because this person transcends all finite being is he capable of being immanent to each being. But for Teilhard and all true, believing Christians, there is only one person who has been inserted into the human race and is capable of drawing other human beings by a human act of love, yet who remains completely transcendent to all human beings. This person must be infinite in order to command the aspirations of all persons for all times. But the only infinite person drawn from among all human beings is Jesus Christ, the God-Man.

Teilhard does not wish to speak of another Christ, a second Christ, different from the first who lived historically in space and time, who "dwelt among us." He intends to speak of the same Jesus Christ of Nazareth, the God-Man, who disclosed Himself to us under a new form and a new dimension.

COSMIC OR CHRISTIC NATURE

Teilhard complains in his unedited work, *Le Christique* (1955) that up to the present, despite the dominant place that St. Paul gives it in his vision of Christ's presence in the world, the third aspect or third "nature" of Christ, has not been given sufficient consideration by theologians. He does not wish to establish a new third nature as opposing the human and divine natures of the one person, Jesus Christ, God made Man. He refers to the "cosmic" function of Christ in the universe, made possible after His death and resurrection through the outpouring of the Holy Spirit. This is the same aspect of Christ that St. Paul constantly writes about, the full, total Christ whose activity consists precisely in "recapitulation" or in bringing the universe to its ultimate center through the transforming energies of Christ's resurrection. [14]

Teilhard, in using the term cosmic or christic "nature" of Christ, does not intend to refer to a new and distinct nature different than that of the risen Lord Jesus. He strongly emphasizes the building up of the Mystical Body of Christ, as a physical "third nature." He claims that this is the meaning of Paul and John and the early Eastern Fathers. The Body of Christ meant for them a living and moving organism wherein we as members were united in a physical and biological sense. [15]

THE BODY OF CHRIST: THE CHURCH — A PHYLUM OF LOVE

To every believer in God, the statement that all human progress is in the final analysis a work of God seems self-evident. But to imagine an indefinite human progress that God would allow for no purpose would be a shocking effrontery to His transcendent dominion over all creatures and His infinite loving goodness toward those whom He created according to His own image and likeness. God bestows His divine filiation on us human beings always gratuitously, but does so in the context of our human development.

This does not mean, however, that the building up of the supernaturalized Mystical Body of Christ flows necessarily from the high degree of human collectivization achieved in the world. Nor does it mean that the Mystical Body of Christ did not exist in periods of more simple, individualistic societies that had not attained a high degree of social consciousness and technical progress.

Teilhard clearly distinguishes between the human developments and the supernatural insertion into that human structure of the purely gratuitous Kingdom of God. He clearly distinguishes in *Mon Univers* (1918) between the ''natural term of human and cosmic advances'' and ''omega, the supernatural term of the Kingdom of God,'' of the ''Plenitude of Christ.''[16]

This body of christified human persons all live in Christ because they live in agapic, self-emptying love toward others and, therefore, are living for Christ (cf. Mt 25:40: ''. . . insofar as you did this to one of the least of these brothers of mine, you did it to me''). Through such members of Christ, He reaches the rest of the human race and the entire material universe through human creative activities done out of love for God and neighbor and the universe.

The christified, the new Israel's People of God, is a ''phylum of salvation'' that spreads its inner life and hyper-personalism (engendered by the life of the physical Body-Person of Christ) in a movement of greater consciousness, always ascending until the completion of the Body at the end of the world.

BUILDING THE UNIVERSE

We see that Teilhard's vision is not new to the Christian faith. It has merely been eclipsed over centuries of dusty, brocaded vestments and stale incense, in punitive laws based on fear of God, of a privatized devotion to Christ so as to reach personal salvation. His spirituality challenges us to move into the very heart of our material world. There, in the hope of the victory of Christ's resurrection working in us through the Holy Spirit, we live and work as citizens of the universe.

We bring God down from heaven above us to discover the Divine Creator inside His world, working with His children to complete His and our world. Good and evil are not necessarily separated, but are discovered as two forces inside the evolutionary process. We become "cosmic" persons as we are united with an earth process that evolved four and a half billion years ago and has brought us to meet with divine indwelling power the challenges of our planet and universe.

This will change our style of prayer as we become more consciously one with the entire universe around us. In Teilhard's *Divine Milieu* and his *Hymn of the Universe* we find a beautiful collection of spontaneous prayers that flow out ecstatically from the heart of their author. In his "Hymn of Matter," we find a prayer suited to all "cosmic citizens" of an evolving world:

I bless you matter and you I acclaim; not as the pontiffs of science or the moralizing preachers depict you, debased, disfigured — a mass of brute forces and base appetites — but as you reveal yourself to me today, in your totality and your true nature.

You I acclaim as the inexhaustible potentiality for existence and transformation wherein the predestined substance germinates and grows.

I acclaim you as the universal power which brings together and unites, through which the multitudinous monads are bound together and in which they all converge on the way of the spirit.

I acclaim you as the melodious fountain of water whence spring the souls of men and as the limpid crystal whereof is fashioned the new Jerusalem.

I acclaim you as the divine milieu, charged with creative power, as the ocean stirred by the Spirit, as the clay molded and infused with life by the incarnate Word. [17]

What a serious responsibility for Christians to take the lead in all fields of human endeavors, knowing with the certainty of God's revelation in Christ Jesus through His Body, the Church, that the world is already "christic." Yet we are called to fashion the universe still more into the total cosmic Christ. Charged with the living presence of Christ within us, we christified human beings live within an expanding universe. We extend the process of christification to hasten the day when the lines of the evolving universe and the evolving Christ in His members will converge in the Omega Point. Then Christ will truly be "all things in all."

As he is the Beginning,
he was first to be born from the
dead,
so that he should be first in every
way;
because God wanted all perfection
to be found in him
and all things to be reconciled

through him and for him,
everything in heaven and everything
on earth,
when he made peace
by his death on the cross
(Col 1:18-20).

BUILDING THE EARTH

There is so much that has been omitted in synthesizing Teilhard's christic vision of the universe. Many excellent works have dealt with this topic.[18] But what has been here presented will allow us to go forth and flesh out more specific areas of our Christian new age consciousness.

I would like to close this chapter with Teilhard's rousing invocation from his work, *The Divine Milieu:*

Jerusalem, lift up your head. Look at the immense crowds of those who build and those who seek. All over the world, men are toiling — in laboratories, in studios, in deserts, in factories, in the vast social crucible. The ferment that is taking place by their instrumentality in art and science and thought is happening for your sake. Open, then, your arms and your heart, like Christ your Lord, and welcome the waters, the flood and the sap of humanity. Accept it, this sap — for, without its baptism, you will wither, without desire, like a flower out of water; and tend it, since, without your own sun, it will disperse itself wildly in sterile shoots.

The temptations of too large a world, the seductions of too beautiful a world — where are these now?

They do not exist.

Now the earth can certainly clasp me in her giant arms. She can swell me with her life, or draw me back into her dust. She can deck herself with every charm, with every horror, with every mystery. She can intoxicate me with her perfume of tangibility and unity. She can cast me to my knees in expectation of what is maturing in her breast.

But her enchantments can no longer do me harm, since she has become for me, over and above herself, the body of Him who is and of Him who is coming.

The divine milieu. [19]

6

A New Psychological Age

Dr. Carl G. Jung called the world religions "the world's great psychotherapeutic symbol systems."[1] But he lamented the fact that religions, especially those in the West, became frozen into a static understanding of the world and no longer provide symbol systems in accord with our modern scientific knowledge. He believed our religious symbols are a response to our level of developed consciousness.

He hoped that a new age would come about, as he wrote in his book, *Aion,*[2] whereby the Christian Churches could provide a new symbolic system to replace the Age of Pisces, symbolized in astrological signs as two fish swimming in different directions. From a world that was represented by two forces in opposition to each other, a world split between the conscious and the unconscious, Jung hoped for a new age that would bring into harmony a union of opposites which he called the "Christification of many."

Jung often spoke in his later writings of a movement today into an Aquarian Age. This astrological sign pictures a man carrying a pail of water. Water is an archetypal symbol of the unconscious. Will this new age bring about a synchronistic age of union between the hidden, potential, dark world of the unconscious, which Jung considered to be a gold mine of untapped richness, and the human world of the conscious?

I will be primarily discussing Jungian psychology in this chapter. There are an almost infinite number of psychological schools, ranging from Freudialism to behaviorism to humanistic psychology to the latest pop psychology fad. These present a wide array of errors and shortcomings in ethics, theology, spirituality, etc. This book, however, is not the place for a detailed critique of them. Of the various schools of psychology, I believe the Jungians provide the most insights that are compatible with Christian spirituality.

Let us, therefore, now seek to draw out the best qualities in modern depth psychology and religion, especially in Christianity, in order to see the necessity and possibility of creating a marriage between the two toward a movement to create a greater new age.

NEED OF RELIGION AND DEPTH PSYCHOLOGY

No true ''new age'' consciousness can come about without a greater complementarity between modern depth psychology and religion. The possibility of a truly ''new age'' thinking is already bursting in upon us, even though most ordinary persons, even so-called ''religious'' persons and even professionals in the various fields of psychology, may not have yet seen this movement already afoot. This begins as an interdiscipline between the ancient wisdom and authentic practices of religion and that of modern depth psychology. It is a great grace for us living at this time in human history to come into such a new synthesis.

This does not mean that individuals in times past did not explore the depths of the unconscious and push their habitual level of consciousness to greater intensity, integrity and fullness of what it means to be a human person. Surely the true mystics down through the centuries stand as those fearless persons, led by the Spirit of God's overshadowing love, who did not fear to push their consciousness to deeper levels to actuate the hidden treasures of their unique personhood locked in the dark abysses of their unconscious.

Dr. Carl G. Jung saw the need for us to know ourselves and the inner working of our psyches. He spoke these words in 1959 on a BBC telecast:

> *One thing is sure — a great change of psychological attitude is imminent. That is certain. And why? Because we need more psychology. We need more understanding of human nature, because the only real danger that exists is man himself. He is the real danger, and we are pitifully unaware of it. We know nothing of man — far too little. His psyche should be studied, because we are the origin of all coming evil.*

Today modern psychology can be a great help to us, for an understanding both of the working of our psyche, and of the "place" where, in inner attentiveness and loving prayer, we can confront our false self and the destructive elements deeply ingrained in our unconscious and find healing and wholeness. But it is also in the unconscious of our psyche that we can experience immediately and directly through God's "numinous" presence, inside of matter and spirit, the distant outline of our true self in our oneness with the *ONE*.

CONSCIOUSNESS ORIGINATES IN THE UNCONSCIOUS

Jung gives us a basic principle that consciousness originates in the unconscious. But, we may ask ourselves, just what is the conscious and the unconscious? With so much discussion today about consciousness expanded to a oneness with God and the universe, we need to define its meaning. Is it something intellectual that we can acquire by taking a seminar or reading a self-help book, thus raising our mental and spiritual level? Is it merely a higher state of neural functioning? And, if so, are there techniques to develop such functioning? Or is it an inner light on which we focus in order to see objects in greater detail, as with bifocals, to aid our limited vision?

Dr. Arthur Diekman defines consciousness as "awareness," rather than the things of which we are aware.[3] It is a common mistake to think of consciousness as self-reflection or introspection of some sort. Consciousness primarily is not this ability to "bend back" upon oneself in reflection. It is primarily a simple, internal experience of oneself and one's activities of sensing, feeling, thinking, judging, reflecting, deciding and acting.[4]

Consciousness is more than to know an object. It is basically not the presence of an object to a subject, but the simple presence in non-reflective awareness of the subject to himself/herself. There are different levels of conscious functioning.[5]

At the lowest level of such functioning dreaming occurs. Next comes the level of sense experience, of seeing, hearing, touching, tasting and smelling. Then follows the level of understanding, of insight, of theory, of hypothesis and of conceptualizing. Beyond this level there occurs the level of reflection, or weighing evidence and of judging. The three levels of experiencing, understanding and judging comprise the basic stages of the knowing process.

But consciousness must not be limited to the level of knowing alone. Beyond the level of knowing there is the level of deliberation, of feeling, of conscious response to values, of decision and of action. Finally, there is the higher level, the graced level of being in intimate love with God. This level embraces ordinary, conscious, God-inspired acts of faith, hope and love, as well as many mystical experiences that Dr. Roberto Assagioli calls "Superconscious."[6]

UNCONSCIOUS

In the strict meaning of the term according to the Freudian school, the unconscious embraces the psychic zone that contains repressed images, memories, thoughts and other materials which cannot be recalled at will without special therapeutic help or the occurrence of special healing events, which can trigger their release. This is called the "personal unconscious."

Underlying this layer is a dark, volcanic base bringing the individual into primordial contact with all of creation as a part to a whole. This Jung calls the "collective unconscious" of the Universal Man. It releases certain images that Jung calls "archetypes." Emotional content connected with these archetypes can powerfully affect our mind in many ways.

Thus we see that the unconscious is a seething mass of primitive images, passion, hate and resentment. In dreams and in insanity the veil is partly drawn aside. But this veil can be pulled aside also by such techniques as hypnosis, drugs, psychotherapy, etc. Deep prayers in the presence of an immanent God can also lead us into this inner world and bring about inner healing and integration of the unconscious with the conscious.

If we are to have an integrated personality, to harmonize all the various levels of psychic life within our minds (a process Jung calls *individuation*), our upper layers of the psyche must be harmonized with the lower layers. This means that the lower layers must be opened up to the scrutiny of our consciousness. We will always remain crippled and a victim of primordial factors in our lives unless we can open up these lower layers and bring there a healing, personalized, loving power.

PRIMORDIAL EXPERIENCES

Dr. Ann Belford Ulanov in her book, *Religion and the Unconscious,*[7] shows that, although depth psychology and Christian theology have different approaches and methodologies, yet "they share a concentration on the hidden depths of human experience and a determination to probe these depths. They go beyond their differences to an intermingling of styles, techniques, and procedures in their common concern with that special kind of human experience which we think is best called *primordial experience.*"[8]

Both religion and depth psychology deal with the ways by which we live and understand the primordial elements of our being. The two disciplines focus on our experiences of meaning and value, but each examines such primary experiences with all the tools available to its own discipline.

Authentic religion has the power to move the believer away from the cultural coding that permits traditions to become fixed and impersonal. Such "traditional religion" operates solely on the secondary process of directive, conscious thinking and cuts off any true progress. True religion allows the individual to move into the hidden areas of the unconscious to make contact with one's genetic coding that is grounded in the numinous and sacred presence of God. This fiery presence of God, the Source of all being, is present within the human unconscious and is locked into the matrix of each atom and subatomic particle. It becomes present, but not as an object to be manipulated by our human consciousness, so basically prone toward self-seeking. Rather, it becomes present as the Creator brings forth through His Logos the uniqueness of the individual person according to God's own image and likeness.

UNION BETWEEN THE CONSCIOUSNESS AND THE UNCONSCIOUS

This is the first great challenge of both depth psychology and religion, especially Christianity: to bring together their own disciplines and methodologies to effect by complementary cooperation a union between human consciousness and the unconscious.

Such a synergy will be the major thrust in our 21st century to create a new age thinking that will allow human beings to grow into greater consciousness of loving oneness with each other and the entire material cosmos. By drawing upon the unlimited riches of the unconscious for extended consciousness, religion and depth psychology can help all of us enter into primordial, religious experiences that will give us conscious knowledge of unending beauty and open up energies to create a new world.

MYTHS, SYMBOLS AND SACRAMENTS

A second major challenge to depth psychology and religion, especially Christianity, is to aid us moderns to recapture the language of the unconscious, namely, myths, symbols and sacraments. The means to effect a creative union between the unconscious and the conscious is through myths and symbols. In the West, Jung complained, we have lost the ability to attain knowledge other than by means of our human intellect. The whole world, therefore, of our conscious mind making contact with the world of the unconscious is lost to most of us. We have lost the ability of children to enter into the primordial and numinous world of the unconscious through the language of myth and symbol.

When we hear the word, *myth*, we think of a fantasy, a mere story to tell children. It does not deal with the harsh world of sense knowledge where a rose is nothing more than a rose.

But there is a deeper meaning to myth that refers to a story that is very much true, even more true at times than "scientific, objective" knowledge. The Bible is full of myths. Ancient cultures had their myths that allowed them to hand down in story form the great human values and ultimate religious meaning to their human lives that could not have been expressed in abstract terms. Jung said to this point: "A tribe's mythology is its living religion, whose loss is always and everywhere, even among the civilized, a moral catastrophe."[9]

Mircea Eliade, the historian of comparative religions in his work, *Myth and Reality*, shows how scholars no longer view a myth as a "fable" or even as "fiction." Rather, myth is accepted as it was in primitive societies, as not only a "true story," but, "beyond that, a story that is a most precious possession because it is sacred, exemplary, significant."[10]

Myths give us models for human behavior in the perennial conflicts between good and evil, by giving deeper meaning and values to human existence. They also destroy the power of *time* by bringing us back to a perfection and completion at the beginning of time. Myth and ritual allowed ancient cultures to "recall" in a sacred *anamnesis* and reenact God's time of perfect harmony. God's eternal plan is first in the finality of creation and comes from all eternity, before the ravages of time. The myths of creation that abound in all cultures, as we see typified by the Jewish story of creation in Genesis, gave the means to celebrate in myth and ritual. They did this by transcending the finite to enter into the unchangeable and the perfect of the divine as the beginning and the goal of all reality.

SYMBOLS

The word, *symbol*, comes from the Greek verb, *symbollein*, meaning to bring or throw together. A symbol brings together two realities, the conscious and the unconscious, and exposes us to new knowledge that goes beyond the limitations of human reason. Jung writes: "As the mind explores the symbol it is led to ideas that lie beyond the grasp of reason."[11] Signs are often invented by a given culture and lack a universal knowledge open to people of all cultures. Symbols are linked to the archetypal, primordial experiences that are not learned by human beings, but are given and recognized universally almost as it were by instinct.

The chief characteristic of a symbol is to make present a hidden reality and to allow human beings to participate in the represented reality. A symbol is a "pointer," but also partakes in the truth it points towards and effects the revelation of that reality. The language of depth psychology and authentic religion is to use symbols to lead persons into primordial experiences of the inner world of the unconscious. When psychology and religion lose the ability to mediate the primordial religious experience of the unconscious through symbols, they lose the possibility of being agents for healing and integration of the conscious and unconscious.

When dogmas are divorced from the symbolic world, religion and psychology become a dehumanized and destructive force, locking the individual into an infantile relation to the psychotherapist or God. But when dogmas and rituals are seen as parts of symbolic language, then they aid in the unification of the conscious and the unconscious.

Jung saw that symbols and the union of the conscious and the unconscious aided in bringing the conscious *ego* in relation to the larger reality of the *self* that could be developed only in relation to the "other." Gabriel Marcel, the philosopher of personalism, repeats over and over in his writings: "The 'I' is the child of the we." We cannot attain true personhood as a unique person except in and through a community of a loving person or persons. It is love that unites and yet differentiates the two lovers into their unique, personal "self."

We are intrinsically bound up with others for our uniqueness.[12] The power of symbols is first that they lead us into the unconscious, where we experience our oneness in history with all other human beings. But, beyond that, symbols hurl us into the very heart of God as a community of Father, Son and Holy Spirit, all emptying themselves in personal self-giving on behalf of each of us.

DREAMS

Jung and his followers have shown how to interpret the various symbols occurring in dreams and how (as Scripture also teaches us) dreams are indispensable tools for self-knowledge. Dreams are means of listening to God as He advises, corrects, punishes, comforts, heals and warns us. God's communication to us is the prime purpose why we dream. It is for us to tune into this valuable way of listening to God beyond our own reasoning.

In such communications God speaks in images, a pictorial, sensual language, that is non-verbal and pre-logical. Dr. Maria Mahoney insists that the unconscious launches a dream to ''wake up'' the dreamer to some aspect of his or her conscious life or personal attitudes about which he or she is sound asleep. [12]

A study of our dreams through recording them in a journal can become an important means of growing in a ''listening'' to God act deeply within our interior. Dr. Ira Progoff gives through his *Journal Workshop* a practical method for using the ''intensive Journal,'' especially to record dreams and other material that might arise from the unconscious when the mind is stilled. [14]

SACRAMENTS

Sacraments are religious rituals that are symbols or outward signs which actively effect a meeting with the Divine. They are signs of inner grace, bringing healing and integration in an immanent union with God. Christians can see the danger of sacraments when they are celebrated ritually, only on a secondary conscious level. They are then divorced from the unconscious, wherein alone the deepest reaches of God as self-giving grace are met in primordial experience of the numinous.

Many modern psychologists and religious teachers of

Hinduism and Buddhism speak of Jesus Christ as a symbol of a Christ-consciousness that represents an integrated human person.

Edward F. Edinger, a Jungian analyst, presents Jesus Christ as a universal symbol of the archetype of the individual ego. Jesus becomes a model for an ideal ego that separates itself from the larger, unconscious, "objective" psyche. Once established in its own ego identity, it finds a way back into relation with the larger *self.* He writes: "The image of Christ gives us a vivid picture of the Self-oriented ego, i.e., the individuated ego which is conscious of being directed by the Self."[15]

For Edinger the incarnation comes about through a *kenosis*, or self-emptying love that St. Paul describes in Philippians 2:6ff. This kenotic process, climaxed in Christ's death on the cross, Edinger sees as the original identification of the ego with the self to attain a limited, but actual existence in space and time. This he claims is what Christ praised in the Beatitudes. Only the emptied ego becomes blessed since it alone can be filled by becoming connected with the riches of the unconscious part of the psyche where the self lives and grows.[16]

JESUS AS SACRAMENT

The Eastern Orthodox Christians and Roman Catholics consider Jesus Christ, God become man, as *the* primordial sacrament. A Christian sacrament is a sacred sign made up of words and actions, employing material symbols in which Jesus Christ desires to meet us in our own time and place in history and to bestow upon us an increase of His divine life. We celebrate our new divine life in Him. But also He communicates that divine life to us as we, in faith, hope and love, open ourselves to Him in such a liturgical encounter.

Jesus Christ, as sacrament, extends His historical person, now glorified and made present through the Church's sacraments, into our history. He connects our outer life with our inner life. In such a true religious experience He brings deep healing and integration of our ego and our self.

The true value of sacraments is that they connect God's inbreaking grace with our own time and space. By receiving Jesus Christ, God-Man, divine and human, we experience both the otherness of God in His awesome and frightening presence (Rudolf Otto's *mysterium tremendum*) and His tender, intimate, nearness in His immanent indwelling, both within our conscious and unconscious minds.

We receive the material symbol of bread and wine in the Eucharist, through faith in the Church as the historical extension of the risen Lord as Head of His Body. We believe that we consciously and openly experience a real encounter with the God-Man and the family of God, the Trinity, on various levels of the unconscious. Open to the operations of God's personalized Spirit of love, on all levels of our being, we experience the living archetype of self-emptying love for each of us as uniquely individuated persons as we are healed and integrated into a oneness with the Divine.

ETHICS REVISITED

A most important challenge that depth psychology holds out to Christianity is that of reexamining the field of ethics in the light of the interaction between the conscious and unconscious levels of an individual. Ethics is the field of philosophy that deals with the moral values which direct us in our choices between what we perceive as right or wrong, good or evil, our duties and obligations according to justice. Ethics embraces the principles that help form our conscience: the disciplines, rules and areas of conflict involved in choosing between right and wrong.

Depth psychology challenges a system of ethics that is based on a static natural law. This system tried to give absolute certitude for peoples of all times, irrespective of the culture in which they lived. Now we all are much more aware of the power of the forces locked within the unconscious to influence deeply what we think and do and say. Therefore, how we evaluate our free deliberation before so many changing factors influencing us in our choices becomes an important part of ethics today.

Today we must reject both relativism and any static norm of conduct or religious "perfection," that separates the consciousness from the unconscious of the individual person. An example of the power of the personal unconscious to influence what may seem to be conscious actions is seen in the case of adults who were beaten and sexually abused in early childhood. They often do to their children what was done to them. How does one form a correct moral judgment on such a person, so powerfully influenced by forces not freely willed by the individual?

We need to accept the existence and active role of unconscious forces if we are to build a realistic ethical system. Dr. Ann Ulanov strongly expresses this reality:

> *By pointing to the unconscious dynamics that underlie all ethical choices and value systems, depth psychology exposes the emptiness of any morality that is separated from the struggles of consciousness and the unconscious, which is to say, of subject and object. Only through the full disclosure of the subjective dimension can we reach objective values, values that will withstand the terrible assaults of human suffering and support us through them.* [17]

In a way, what seems to be a "new ethics" is really what has been taught and practiced for centuries in Western Christianity. One must form one's conscience according to one's level of freedom and knowledge of the concrete human situation. What seems to be new is a movement away from an ethics that offered a code of perfection as extrinsic and indifferent to the history of the individual person. All persons from all times were to conform to such a norm of action. This so often led to repressing consciously or unconsciously all impulses, needs or desires that would not fit into such an ethics.

An unhealthy asceticism was encouraged that furthered such repressions with very serious repercussions as the smoldering volcanic material lying in the unconscious boomeranged and took its revenge through neuroses and psychoses. The new ethics looks, not so much to a goal of perfection to be attained equally by all, but to *wholeness*. The ego no longer identifies solely with an extrinsic moral code, but sees it as only a part, even though an essential one, of the larger self that includes the unconscious as well as the conscious parts of the psyche.

SUFFERING, EVIL AND SALVATION

Religion and psychology both deal with human values that stretch out to ultimate finality in searching for answers to what it means to be a fully realized human being. A challenge for both disciplines to create a new age consciousness comes from the perennial problems of why there are so many evils and sufferings in our world. Do these have any human value? What does salvation mean in the light of suffering and evil? Living in an age that puts faith in science to solve all human problems, we can see that religion and depth psychology must play a key role in opening us moderns to another approach that goes beyond any trite and inadequate rational answer as the only possible approach.

The German poet, Rainer Maria Rilke, in his poem, ''To Live Everything,'' provides a deep insight for Christians who seek a rational answer to so perplexing a problem:

Be patient toward all that is
unsolved
in your heart. . . .
Try to love the questions
themselves. . . .
Do not now seek the answers,
which cannot be given because
you would not be able to live them.
And the point is,
to live everything.
Live the questions now.
Perhaps you will then,
gradually,
without noticing it,
Live along some distant day
into the answers.

VARIOUS APPROACHES TO SUFFERING

Some religions and cultures saw sufferings and evils as inevitable. Death was considered a liberation, a blessing whereby human beings could escape such unpreventable sufferings. Some, like the Stoics, sought to master suffering through a grim asceticism that rendered them insensitive to pain, but also towards others. Others revolted against a God who would allow such evils and sufferings. Other religions encouraged the faithful passively to resign and endure such sufferings since there would be a future reward for them in a heavenly existence to come.

Today psychology gives religion many new values and insights into the universal problems of suffering and evil.

Psychology needs to bring a healing hopefulness to persons undergoing sufferings on the physical, psychological and spiritual levels. Real suffering breaks up our security system that both society with its cultural coding, as well as our own false ego, have fashioned into a steel-encased fortress of isolation from others, including God. Psychotherapists must be challenged to move beyond their oedipal myths and others to become authentic ministers of hope and healing.

Neurosis is one form of psychic revolt that brings with it an army of psychosomatic sicknesses. Psychotherapy methods must not be employed only to bring some limited relief from symptoms through analysis. Other methods must be found by psychotherapists to seek to help patients find hope through a new positive experience of themselves as unique, beautiful and creative persons.

Christianity must be challenged to cooperate with psychology in aiding the faithful through its traditional myths, symbols and sacraments to become more aware of their unconscious, hidden realities and potentialities for good. Priests and ministers can play an essential role, especially in pastoral counseling and in preaching and celebrating the sacred rituals. By doing so, they can help the faithful to find the divine presence positively working out of the unconscious to bring forth creative, individuated persons with a cosmic sense of belonging to the universe and contributing to its rich development in terms of highest moral values.

JESUS — SOURCE OF HOPE

Christianity builds its uniqueness on the belief that Jesus Christ is truly God, the second person of the Trinity, who freely takes on our humanity and all that this implies. He enters into our sufferings and into His own unconscious that ties Him irrevocably and forever with us human beings, both with the personal experiences of sufferings and evils in His lifetime, but also with the collective unconscious.

Jesus encounters evil wherever He finds it and His strategy is to invite His listeners to accept, not the mere hope of some external happiness in the life to come, but Himself as the *way* to greater, unending life, even now experienced in personal integration. He insisted to his hearers that the only answer to the problem of sufferings stemming from seen and unseen evils is to follow Him into true life.

Like a warrior leaping into battle, so Jesus approached the problem of evil and the concomitant sufferings as a warfare against inimical powers. Sin is more for Jesus than what individual persons freely and deliberately commit against God's commands. The mystery of evil invades deeply within the human unconscious, but also throughout the cosmic strata. It was precisely the collective mystery of evil that Jesus encountered during His human existence on this earth. He conquered it by His inner oneness with His all-holy Father and with the Spirit of self-emptying love.

A DIVINE SYNERGY

Jesus reveals an inner consciousness of His ultimate worth and meaning as one who derives all meaningfulness from His complete dependence upon the Father, as the Source of His being. There is no vanity or self-seeking in His words or actions. His primal motivation is to return the infinite love He receives from the Father by serving His wishes. He lives in His loving presence, as He becomes more and more surrendering in each moment to the working of His Father in His life. "My Father goes on working, and so do I" (Jn 5:17). As the Father loves Him and serves Him in all things, so Jesus loves us and serves us (Jn 15:9).

By becoming more consciously one in union with the divine community of indwelling, self-emptying Father, Son and Holy Spirit, we Christians will not find any answer to *why* we have to suffer and why there are evils in this world that all of us, especially the innocent, seemingly must suffer. But we will be given the inner strength by faith, hope and love, gifts from God, to surrender to a loving power that seeks only our complete happiness.

JOURNEY INWARD

Dag Hammarskjold writes in his diary:

The longest journey
Is the journey inward
Of him who has chosen his destiny
Who has started his quest
For the source of his being. [18]

True religion and true psychology can best prepare us for entrance into a Christian New Age consciousness by facilitating us, each by its special methods and disciplines, in our most important journey through the labyrinthine darkness where ultimately we meet Light in "luminous darkness," to quote St. Gregory of Nyssa of the 4th century. Such inner solitude, where we learn to leave the outside, flattering, pampering world of the senses and illusions, can come about only if we have the courage to taste our inner poverty.

There is a great paradox about making a wedding between the consciousness and the elements locked inside our unconscious. Giving up the insecurities we mistook for our sole securities, we find absolute security in the Absolute Being of our being. By forcing ourselves into such inner sufferings and confrontation with seeming chaotic evil, we prepare ourselves to meet God as Divinity, emptied to take upon Himself our broken humanity in the person of the historical God made man, Jesus Christ.

Then we Christians will understand what St. Paul meant about the "new creation" and our role creatively to bring this about:

*If then any person is in Christ, he
is a new creature;
the former things have passed away;
behold, they are made new!
But all things are from God, who has
reconciled us to himself
through Christ and has given us
the ministry of reconciliation
(2 Cor 5:17-18).*

7

The Role of Christianity In Building A Better World

We all seek desperately for peace. We desire peace and harmony within our individual selves, within our family, among friends and neighbors, in our cities, state, country and throughout the entire world. Yet with the Prophet Jeremiah we too can say: " 'Peace! Peace!' they say, but there is no peace. They should be ashamed of their abominable deeds, but they are not" (Jr 6:14).

In the Old Testament, the Hebrew word for peace, *shalom*, connotes the sense of being whole, intact, finished, complete. The noun means chiefly a state of well-being, health, prosperity, numerous offspring, a long life, victory over one's enemies and peaceful possession of the Promised Land. It refers not only to the individual's peace, but also to peace given to the collective people of God as a nation.

God so loved the world as to give us His only Son, so that whoever would believe in Him, would have eternal life (Jn 3:16). Jesus came not merely to speak to us about peace; as the Word of God, He creates peace. He acts to bring peace to individuals through His healing love and through His disciples to extend such peaceful harmony throughout the world. "For God is a God of

— 143 —

peace, not disorder'' (Rm 14:33). ''God has called us to peace'' (1 Cor 7:15).

Yet this peace, which He alone can give, cannot be had without a deep upheaval of all our carnal values that flow out of our sinful self-centeredness. To follow Jesus' way that alone brings true peace, there is need of violence to whatever opposes our living in complete, loving submission to God and in loving our neighbor as we love ourselves. ''Do not think that I have come to send peace upon the earth; I have come to bring a sword, not peace'' (Mt 10:34).

Christ, the true Prince of Peace, is a sign that is spoken against (Lk 2:34). His peace brings no comfort to our sinful tendencies to cling to the illusory world. We have created such a world in order to remain in our false securities to which we cling because we fear to surrender in trust to a God we cannot see but whom we foolishly think we can control with our minds.

THE ROLE OF THE CHURCH

The Church is the extension of the risen Lord Jesus into our present time and place of human history. The mission of the Church is to lead, not only Christians, but all men and women of good will to develop peace, *shalom.* That is to say, the Church's mission is one of integration and development of the earth's potential and the granting of human dignity to every person, made by God according to His own image and likeness (Gn 1:26).

Pope Paul VI in his important encyclical on *The Development of Peoples (Populorum Progressio,* issued March 26, 1967) insisted that to create world peace is a work for all human beings, by being engaged in development of the earth's resources into a world community based on love and justice. We see a world that is divided into two parts. One is made up of an elite of free persons who enjoy wealth, security and freedom. The majority of human beings live lives of extreme poverty and lack of decent employment.

Today we are able to reflect through social sciences and the laws of economics to see how destructive human societies become when they are ruled by a powerful few. We are all responsible for developing a world where everyone can enjoy basic needs, freedoms and a proper dignity, befitting children of the one true God.

THE SIN OF THE WORLD

The Book of Genesis gives us an account of the reality of sin that first entered into the human race when man freely broke the social oneness that he was meant to enjoy with God and other human beings. Original sin is more than the first, personal sin of the first human being, that is then juridically imputed to every human being thereafter born. It is the first sin and each personal sin of every human being that has ever lived, including you and me. But it adds to itself a oneness that we all share with an alienated human community. We are all united in our broken condition and alienated from God and from each other and from the material cosmos.

It is a cosmic "groaning" together in "slavery to decadence," as St. Paul writes (Rm 8:21). A. Hulsbosch described this community-solidarity: "Sin has taken root in the human community, in order to rule over it as a tyrannizing power. Whoever is born into this community is irrevocably delivered to this power."[1]

COLLECTIVE GUILT

We, as human beings made in the likeness of God's own image and loved infinitely by God through Jesus Christ in His Spirit, cannot merely be content with changing our inner perception and think we will be one with all human beings in peace and justice. Because collective sin has invaded into the human situation to produce structures of sin, evil does not merely exist in our own inner perception of a disunited world. One focus of change will be our struggle to destroy our own personal involvement in adding to separation and division.

That will necessitate a constant *praxis* or inner attention in the ascetical order of changing our thought pattern from one of self-centeredness and separation from others, to one of loving oneness in service. But it will also require our constant involvement to change the social structures of sin.

As we see the mighty weight of social, economic and political structures in shaping conscience, we cannot change our perceptions unless we labor also in a social reform to change the structures that feed into our perceptions a ''sinful'' attitude toward society. We imbibe ''sin'' from our environment that in a way precedes and conditions our every conscious choice. We accept the sinful *status quo* as ''business as usual.'' And as we live, so does the Church, since we are the Church.

One of the greatest forces of evil in our modern world stems from collectivization. As the family and clan developed into a village, town, city, state, country and nation and allied countries, the individual yielded his/her moral decisions to the im-personalized group. Groups are not primarily organized for evil, but gradually there usually results a tendency toward what Professor Irving Janis of Yale University coins as ''group-think.''[2]

Such ''sinfulness'' shows itself in the group as a whole, feeling infallible. This has been seen in corporate evil perpetrated by the Church throughout its history as it sacralized certain political structures in its cooperation with state-nations. Any action it unanimously agreed on would automatically have been considered as good and blessed by God. The ''sacred'' group, so the thinking went, always looks out for the greatest good. In such thinking the enemy of the Church and of God always thinks differently from the holy group, and such an enemy is basically evil. Fighting such an enemy is to help God in enforcing righteousness.

GOD THINKS AS WE DO

This thinking drove Jesus to the cross. Such rationalization allowed white men to kill 100,000 Indians in California alone between 1820 and 1850. God, so they thought, is on the side of them, the white men, "in whom there is no darkness." Thus they could develop the slave trade in which thousands of defenseless blacks from African villages (more often than not already enslaved by fellow Africans) were herded as brute animals into the holes of ships, chained in their excretions, and then sold to farmers, "genteel" Christian folk, politicians, priests and nuns, to be their slaves.

Hitler could whip a nation of Christians into immobility as he ordered six million Jews and millions of other "undesirables" to be killed. Stalin and Mao killed countless millions. Turks could wipe out a million and a half Armenians. In our own days nearly a million in Cambodia have seen death. Still no one seems very perturbed, including Christians, around the world! Who can number the millions of aborted babies murdered in clinics that offer abortions on demand? Millions have been dying of starvation in the sub-Saharan countries of Africa and we as a group hear it once and then get on with earning more money for our rich nations.

One of our greatest industries is supplying arms to any nation, even to two nations in deadly combat, who destroy themselves while we become "fatter" by their hateful holocausts. Americans and Soviets have nuclear destructive power to annihilate the planet ten times over and still there is no sensible control or disarmament of nuclear arms.

But perhaps our duplicity is mostly seen in great American corporations, entering undeveloped countries to bring them "salvation" by setting up factories and plants to exhaust the resources of such countries in huge dividends that end up in the pocket of the few stockholders back home. The rich become richer and the poor become poorer and more oppressed by those who "have."

SINS OF COLLECTIVE "RELIGION"

The evils that individuals have perpetrated in the name of God and religion cannot compare with the "institutionalized" evils inflicted upon innocent people in the name of religion. What hatred and violent persecutions Christians in the name of their meek Lamb of God have inflicted upon the Jewish people! How many people died through the centuries in so-called "holy wars"!

A NEW CHALLENGE TO CHRISTIANITY

In our modern world Christianity is being given a new challenge to join the forces of men and women of good will to salvage and reconstruct the world. The Church is being called back to its original view as handed down by the first Christian community in Jerusalem and taught by Jesus Christ, its Founder. The Spirit of the risen Jesus is already releasing a dynamism within the Church and among its leaders to carry out its original mission.

No longer can the Church ignore the historical moment the entire world is now passing through. The Church is being invited by such groups as the United Nations, the World Council of Churches and by many other collective activist groups around the world to join in the reconstruction of a new world based on the dignity of every human being.

The suffering countries of the Third World are calling out to the Church to conscientize public opinion in the industrialized nations by reorganizing the world according to greater justice and freedom guaranteed to each human person. The Church is an international organization, unique among such world structures. By Church we do not mean only the hierarchy or the ecclesiastical organization. It embraces all who believe in Jesus Christ and who commit their lives to the faith passed on through traditions and the sacraments. It builds itself up and therefore turns to the world in which such Christians live to create a more just and harmonized world. It does so as its members hear and speak the living Word of God and organize themselves around a hierarchy to carry out what they have heard and experienced.

THE CHURCH
CAN MAKE A GLOBAL CONTRIBUTION

The Catholic Church has been chastened by its sinful coopera-tion as an accomplice to the so-called "Christian" nations in the process of sacralizing or making sacred political, social and economic systems that still hold the majority of human beings in poverty and human indignities. Now it is faced with two alterna-tives. The Church can continue to preach "cheap grace" by passively accepting the political and economic orders of the world. Or it can become a leader of a revolution to throw off the evil vestiges of colonization and communism and to help build a new, just and more humane (and therefore, more truly Christian) world-society.

Pope Paul VI set the stage for the urgent responsibility to be assumed by the followers of Christ to create a better world in his important encyclical, *The Development of Peoples* (issued March 26, 1967). This followed two years after the close of the Second Vatican Council which outlined (especially in its pastoral Constitu-tion on *The Church in the Modern World* and its decrees on religious freedom, ecumenism and relations with non-Christian religions) a renewed consciousness of the demands of the Gospel to be at the service of all by a solidarity of international cooperation.

Prior to the Council, three other Popes raised the consciousness of Christians and non-Christians to the need of a solidarity in action on a global plane to effect greater justice to all human beings on the social, economic, political and religious levels. These pioneers were Leo XIII, Pius XI and John XXIII. Pope John Paul II, especially, most recently has captured the attention of the world through his Herculean trips to all parts of the globe to preach the Gospel values as well as through his outstanding encyclical, *On Social Concern.* [4]

The Catholic Church with its organized parishes, schools, universities and hospitals, found in every country of the world, has a unique role to play in organizing and mobilizing its resources to conscientize those who are ready to listen to the universal values of the Gospel. Many organizations, such as the United Nations and other national groups are turning to the Church to give a universal vision, now untainted by any one national interest or cultural limitation, of the oneness of all human beings under one God over us all.

The Church alone can give a continuity with the past ethical values found in all religions and cultures, and yet stretch the vision of all human beings in a discontinuity that will for the first time in history place the good of the community of the world before the domestic short-term benefits and welfare.

The repentant Church is very aware of the evils of canonizing structures and organizations to perpetuate injustice inflicted upon the majority of human beings by a small, powerful elite. It can best call the nations to repentance for domestic and internal *sins* and highlight the mercy of God to bring about a conversion for a new global order.

ANALYSIS INTO PAST HISTORICAL FACTORS

The first great work needed to effect a radical revolutionary upheaval of existing organizations is to analyze and research how the world situation in which we presently find ourselves came about. Part of that will be to hear the cries of the poor and make an option to help better their plight and thus build a more equitable world.

The needed work will be to pose concrete ways of promoting the development of a better world and how to organize systems to bring this about. Pope Paul VI in his encyclical uses the concept of *development* as the new name for bringing about peace.

> *Excessive economic, social and cultural inequalities among peoples arouse tensions and conflicts, and are a danger to peace. As we said to the Fathers of the Council when we returned from our journey of peace to the United Nations: "The conditions of the peoples in process of development ought to be the object of our consideration; or, better: Our charity for the poor in the world — and there are multitudes of them — must become more considerate, more active, more generous." To wage war on misery and to struggle against injustice is to promote, along with improved conditions, the human and spiritual progress of all men, and therefore the common good of humanity. Peace cannot be limited to a mere absence of war, the result of an ever precarious balance of forces. No, peace is something that is built up day after day, in the pursuit of an order intended by God, which implies a more perfect form of justice among men.* [5]

DEVELOPMENT

Development can never be reduced solely to economic growth. It embraces politics, culture, economics and also religion.

We might think that to create a new international economic order may seem primarily to be the goal of international politics and mutual cooperation among the nations. But for such a social transformation there must first be a dismantling of mental structures that permit one faction to become more prosperous at the expense of the other faction, the helplessly poor and marginalized.

The Church can be most effective in keeping with its primary mission to create a new ethical and spiritual impetus by preaching the Gospel to all, but, above all, to comfort and preach to the poor their human worth. They make their human worth manifest by no longer resigning passively to the powerfully ruling classes, but by having a developed sense of responsibility for self-guidance and for hope.

Father Vincent Cosmao, in his stimulating book, *Changing the World*, well describes the mutual relationship between the Church's call to evangelize and to conscientize both the prosperous and the poor of the world:

> *Neither one being subordinated to the other, the tasks of evangelization and conscientization are so closely bound up that they cannot be dissociated, though it may be useful to distinguish them for purposes of analysis. All the basic processes of church life — preaching, catechesis, pastoral care, and so forth — can and should contribute to conscientization. To the extent that they do, they cannot help but further the desired effect of evangelization: that persons lead their lives in the kind of relationship with God that they seek to inculcate. In de facto experience this convergence or identification of evangelization and development is so clear and obvious that it is useless to prolong the either/or debate that assumes we must choose between the two. A conscientizing evangelization can disturb only those who dread the subversive — creative — power of the gospel message.* [6]

Thus the transformation of the world through development becomes one of the criteria for authenticating our Christian faith. This was highlighted at the 1971 synod of bishops in their document, *Justice in the World*: "Action on behalf of justice and participation in the transformation of the world fully appear to us as a constitutive dimension of the preaching of the Gospel . . . of the Church's mission for the redemption of the human race and its liberation from every oppressive situation."[7]

The Church discovered in recent decades that preaching the Gospel also demanded taking an active role in global development, especially in the underdeveloped countries. Aware of Christ's mission to feed the hungry and clothe the naked, the Church strove as always throughout its history to practice charity in providing for the basic needs of all, wherever they may live and of whatever culture or religion. But it was not far into the 20th century that Church leaders and missionaries saw the urgency to go to the root of the problems of poverty and injustice by actively participating in the transformation of the world order through development.

The Gospel brings a judgment on sin and evil in the world, not to condemn the world, but to bring salvation to it. It has always been the role of the Church to fight injustices wherever they may exist and to attack the roots of any structures in society that continue those injustices. The Church is never more the Church of Christ as when it preaches to the poor the hope of the risen Jesus and the basic relationship of God to His children, made in His own image. True worship of God is active, loving service for all fellow human beings, starting with the poor and the defenseless. The Church needs to develop a social order in which no human being is neglected but everyone has the basic resources to live a dignified human life.

JESUS THE LIBERATOR

God revealed such justice and a way of living (*praxis*) to His Chosen People. The Hebrews of the Old Testament had a keen sense of solidarity and equality with all other members of their society. This was the constant preaching of the prophets when the people turned away from the high ethical living revealed by God for His chosen ones.

And when God's love burst upon our darkened world in the person of Jesus Christ, God enfleshed as man, His ministry was one of announcing the Good News of the Kingdom of God as already happening in and through His person. He also denounced all evils that would obstruct this Kingdom. Jesus was a prophet of hope, who not only gave the message of a new creation, but who became the medium through whom this new creation would come about.

He came to awaken all men and women from their sleep and darkness to move into a new realization. This new consciousness centered on the basic goodness of every human being, but to urge us all to use our talents to take responsibility to help in creating a new world, transformed by God's love operating within and among us.

Jesus was anointed by God to announce the inbreaking of the Kingdom of God as He preached in the synagogue of Nazareth, "to announce good news to the poor, to proclaim release for prisoners and recovery of sight for the blind; to let the broken victims go free, to proclaim the year of the Lord's favor" (Lk 4:16-22; cf. Is 61:1-2). With the coming of God's Kingdom on earth justice would be done at last to the oppressed. God would visit His people and fulfill His promises. He would reign in the world and His kingdom of peace, justice and brotherhood would appear in all its perfection. All the aspirations of mankind would be fulfilled. The world would become what God destined it to be through a total and everlasting liberation and fulfillment.

All God's richness placed inside of His created world would be drawn out by human cooperation and creative action through humble and loving service. It would be a liberation from sin, division, hatred, death and suffering.

CALL TO DECISION

But the fulfillment of God's Kingdom on earth will come about only by our cooperation within the context of our situation. The building up of this Kingdom faces us in our everyday life. It challenges our way of life and concrete attitudes. It calls us to a decision now. None of us, the Church teaches, can escape into unreal dreams. We are held to our earth-bound realities. God meets us and co-creates with us this new world in the historical context of the present world situation.

George Mangatt well summarized the mission of the Church and of every true Christian to bring about this new world harmony and justice:

The kingdom of God Jesus proclaimed is not a purely other-worldly reality to be realized only in the future, but something that has effectively entered into human history, transforming the whole human existence. It does not consist merely in the salvation of the soul, but in the total liberation of the human person from all forms of slavery and affliction, spiritual, material and social. It is God's fatherly rule of mercy, forgiveness, justice and universal love. Where there is any form of slavery, injustice, hatred or oppression there God cannot be ruling, there the Kingdom of God cannot exist. The total human situation — individual, social, economic, political — is assumed into God's rule and Kingdom; where anti-God forces in any form dominate and oppress God's children, God's rule cannot be real. That is why Jesus conceived his mission as an integral liberation of the whole human person; that is why he went about healing the sick, feeding the hungry, freeing the possessed; that is why he fought the injustices of the Jewish aristocracy.[8]

Jesus commissioned His first disciples to go forth and, not merely to announce the good news about the coming of the Kingdom of God, but to bring His healing love and power to all mankind (Mk 16:16-18). Jesus continues to heal the broken of the world and bring about a new age through those who surrender themselves to Him and allow Him to work through them to be a freeing power in their society.

THE EARLY CHURCH

The early Christians were convinced that anyone who was in Christ was already a new creation and God was calling him/her to be a cooperator, a co-creator, a reconciler, as St. Paul says (2 Cor 5:17-18). The words of Thomas Merton aptly summarize the belief and manner of living in the society of early Christian times. "It is only in assuming full responsibility for our world, for our lives and for ourselves that we can be said to live really for God."[9]

The early Christian Fathers realized that the heart of Christianity focused on a deep concern toward the poor, the suffering and the afflicted. They had experienced the infinite love of God in Christ Jesus. This led them into an inner spirit of poverty that could be called humility. They had experienced the compassionate mercy of the Heavenly Father through the incarnate Jesus. It was this divine love that drove them to become incarnate compassion and mercy toward all the poor around them. They realized that poverty and oppression admitted of many levels and manifestations. The most evident was that of physical poverty, for that was the teaching of Jesus (Mt 25:35-40).

With St. James, they knew that faith without good works was dead (Jm 2:15-17). Their deep prayer made them realize that the whole human race formed, in God's designs, one community under one loving Father. God had bequeathed His creation and all creatures, not to a few individuals, but to all mankind. St. Basil of the 4th century speaks of a ''common and universal sharing of possessions. It is lawful for each one to take from these common possessions to the degree that he/she is able and that is suited to the individual person's needs.''[10]

Deep prayer, healing through the sacraments, and a constant vigilance over self-centeredness gave them a keen realization of the need they had of sharing riches with all, especially those in greatest need. All persons had a strict right to the use of what they needed in order to live decently. Those who possessed more of talents and wealth had a need to share these with the poor. The wealthier ones were merely God's administrators or stewards of a common possession given them by God to be distributed to all in need.

St. Ambrose gives the doctrine that was mutually shared by the Western and Eastern Fathers:

> *The Lord our God willed that this earth should be the common property of all mankind and so, He offered its produce for all to enjoy; but man's avarice distributed the right to its possession.*[11]

If, as the Fathers claimed, wealth has no other purpose than that of being shared, it follows that the rich will become less rich materially and they will simply cease to be rich. They were drawing their conclusions from their praying over Scripture, and especially the commands of Jesus to love all as He loves us.

PRAXIS, NOT THEORY

The urgent issue that faces all Christians and non-Christians today is: how can we develop a world society so as to ensure a more equitable, just distribution of necessary goods and services to all so that every human being may live on the physical, psychological and spiritual levels a life of human dignity befitting a child of God? The real question today is whether all human beings can work for true progress according to justice and peace for all.

This is to put on the mind of Christ, who died for all human beings. By His Spirit of love working in us and among us, we can transform society, so that all human beings can in freedom make choices in human dignity to become more and more in the image and likeness of God. All human beings are called by God to such a task. But Christians, especially — through the revelation of God's love manifested in the love of His Son made flesh, who died for all God's children in order to take away sin, selfishness and estrangement from each other — should strive to live in the unity of His Spirit by living in love and service to each other, especially toward those in need. Thus we show the world, not by arguments that God really exists, but we incarnate His love born again as we members live in Christ, our Head.

The Church's mission given by the Son of God is negatively to resist any sacralization of human societies that are based on inequality and injustice. Positively it is to join forces with all who together acknowledge that the one God is love by struggling for peace and justice.

As in early Christianity, so now among all Christians and others of good will, this can come about only by *praxis*, by our participation in a revolution. By working for a reconstruction of disintegrating societies all such workers are also building up the Church, the Body of Christ, and actuating the Kingdom of God, even now on earth. Christian laity and Church leaders, especially by faith to believe in God's Spirit of creative, unifying love, can also believe in the real ability of the Church to surrender to truth and put that truth into practice.

The Church now has its greatest opportunity to set in motion a universal revolution against any systems now exploiting the poor of this world and positively to work for the transformation of the world as the only way to truly praise and worship the hidden God.

> *This, rather, is the sort of fast that pleases me . . . to break unjust fetters and undo the thongs of the yoke, to let the oppressed go free, and break every yoke, to share your bread with the hungry, and shelter the homeless poor, to clothe the man you see to be naked and not turn from your own kin (Is 58:6-7).*

A LIVING, LIBERATING FAITH

The Church must recapture its prophetic role by calling people to acknowledge the ''sin of the world'' and, transformed by God's Spirit of love, to love all others as oneself. God becomes a concerned, compassionate, liberating God wherever human beings work for peace and break the idols of tyrants, posing as false deities.

Today we see, coming out of the Third World, Christian theologians preaching a liberation theology. Because they are sharing the lot of the poor and with them they are listening to God's Word, they are discovering a deeper faith they never knew before. It starts with realizing that they have no liberating power in themselves, but only in God's Word lived. In such inner poverty of spirit and seeming helplessness in human efforts, such theologians are touching the kiss of death and passing over into a new creation by the saving Word of Jesus Christ. Such theologians are mystics and prophets leading others through death to new life. They are a light of resurrectional hope for those who sit in darkness.

In 1948, in article 28 of the *Universal Declaration of Human*

Rights, the United Nations founded its existence and goal on this principle: "Everyone is entitled to a social and international order in which the rights and freedoms set forth in this Declaration can be fully realized." There can never exist a world authority capable of enforcing such a very Christian principle. There can be no ready-made model for a new world order based on equality and justice for all persons.

God has never specified how this new creation would come about, step by step according to a blueprint. But He gave us the guiding principles and His Spirit of love. The same Spirit that brooded over the chaos and void in the Genesis account of creation still hovers over the not-yet. That Spirit, rather than taking us away from the struggles of the world, pushes us deeper into political, economic and social involvement in order to make justice a reality in all human relations.

We cannot turn away from building a more equitable world, because there is no other world possible.

A NEW REVOLUTION

The Church must not turn away from its responsibility to present clear ideas and a theological anthropology according to God's revelation. Its influence internationally must be focused on educating the public to create a political will to change the world into a community of loving service and respect for every human being.

What is called for from the Church is to lead a new kind of revolution. Such a revolution must be directed by negotiation by all parties concerned. The Church must call the world to recognize and act out of the fundamental principle that there is a oneness of all human beings and that the goods of the earth have been given to us for the use of all of us, especially those in greatest need. The Church, by listening to God's Word as it comes especially from

God's poor ones, will be able to open up its unconscious *memory* to hear what God's living Word, Jesus Christ, is saying to His Body. Through His Spirit God opens up to all people of good will a world of infinite creativity.

Christianity in this new age will need no armies and fleets of ships to conquer the world for Christ. But by being the spearhead for a liberation movement against strange gods, it will be the prime, living example of what it means to die to worldly power that always generates injustice, alienation, ignorance and war. The Church will be reborn in its own nakedness as humbly it goes forth to be the suffering servant among all other suffering servants.

Christians, by engaging in self-liberation, will become free to call God their Liberator and bring His freeing power to those prisoners of sinful structures. We will speak of God to the world only as we act out of love and justice in peace in the world. Any theory or explanation the Church may give must come only after the *praxis* is seen actuated by the Church's "subversive" fighting all forms of injustice. God becomes real to a world only to the degree that His Word is not only heard but eaten, and where those whom He sends prophetically speak by actions that are done out of justice and peace.

8

The Holy Spirit Broods Over The World

From my earliest childhood I have always been fascinated by butterflies. I was always entranced by the beauty and grace of such a creature of God as it danced merrily from flower to flower or, drunken with the sweetness of just being alive, it flitted about in the summer air in a frenzied dance of joyous abandonment. In school I learned about the butterfly's humble origin from a lowly caterpillar, not very beautiful to behold, so slow in its crawling efforts to get somewhere. The beautiful butterfly was being formed even as a caterpillar, but even more so as the caterpillar spun its prison-like confinement and entered into the chrysalis stage. In such womb-tomb confinement, slowly, a new and more beautiful creature was being fashioned.

As the cocoon splits down its sides, the butterfly emerges, wings wet and tightly packed. The wings stretch out and the butterfly flies off — a new creation that hardly resembles the caterpillar. Yet all that beauty and ability to fly were locked in hidden potential within the ugly little caterpillar. I later learned in college biology that those very wings were already present in outline form and basic structure in the caterpillar and pupa stages.

Yet a slow metamorphosis was needed to manifest externally what was already there internally.

This for me has always been a guiding example of the transformation that can take place in the lives of all of us human beings under the power of God's creative Love, the Holy Spirit. From the moment of our conception in our mother's womb, we, too, are launched on a course of evolution. There is a bodily development that is very dependent for its full growth on outside factors, such as the genes of our parents, food, drink and personal loving care.

But there is also in all of us a psychic and spiritual development that requires very much our own loving cooperation if we are to reach new levels of human perfection. God's evolving Spirit of love is operating during our earthly pilgrimage by drawing out on the physical level what has been locked inside of the 100,000 genes in the 23 pairs of chromosomes in conception. The physical genes received gratuitously through our parents and their ancestors dispose us to a continued development guided by God's creative, loving power. This growth will evolve hidden potentials of psychic and spiritual abilities that in our finitude will never know the possibility of stopping an enriching growth, not even in the life to come, provided we individuals cooperate with God's transforming Spirit.

WHO IS THE HOLY SPIRIT?

We speak of man's spirit, the spirit of a football team, the spirit of '76, the Aquarian Age of the spirit, and then there is the *Holy Spirit.* To reach an adequate meaning of the word *spirit,* we need to turn in faith to receive a higher knowledge of God's immanent, creative presence in all of matter than we can conceive by our own limited human knowledge. Once we lived in a world that we separated into two parts. Everything we saw on this earth was labeled animate or inanimate. Living things such as human beings, birds, animals and plants all were "animated" by an inner spirit or soul, as the principle of life. Rocks and solid things like tables and chairs were considered to be static, "life-less," and, therefore, inanimate. They possessed no soul to give them an inner growing and directive force.

Today nuclear physicists speak much like mystics, as Einstein and his followers declare that nothing is static or "dead." Today modern physicists no longer see a severe dichotomy or separation between the spiritual and the physical. Dr. Larry Dossey writes: "Our greatest spiritual achievement may lie in total integration of the spiritual and the physical — in realizing that the spiritual and physical are not two aspects of ourselves, but one. Perhaps the ultimate spiritual goal is to transcend *nothing*, but to realize the oneness of our own being. . ."[1]

THE SPIRIT UNIFIES THE UNIVERSE

Our Christian faith assures us that God, as a trinitarian community of love, explodes in His *kenotic* or self-emptying love to create a world of seemingly infinite diversity. Yet all multiplicity is continually being guided by the loving, overshadowing Holy Spirit to fashion a oneness, the fullness of the Logos of God enfleshed in matter. The Spirit is moving throughout the material world lovingly to draw God's embryonic creation into the definitive unity — the Body of Christ. St. Paul expressed the creative process as terminating in the cosmic Christ. "There is only Christ; he is everything and he is in everything" (Col 3:11).

St. Athanasius in the 4th century expresses such Christian optimism in a world moving toward an ordered beauty and harmony through the Holy Spirit:

Like a musician who has attuned his lyre, and by the artistic blending of low and high and medium tones produces a single melody, so the Wisdom of God, holding the universe like a lyre, adapting things heavenly to things earthly, and earthly things to heavenly, harmonizes them all, and leading them by His will, makes one world and one world order in beauty and harmony. [2]

OVERSHADOWING OF THE HOLY SPIRIT

From the Book of Genesis we see at the beginning of creation by the Trinity, the presence of the Holy Spirit as God's creative power. God's presence as loving Orderer and Harmonizer is seen as His Spirit of love hovering over the chaos and the void like a mighty, cosmic bird. ''Now the earth was a formless void, there was darkness over the deep, and God's spirit hovered over the water'' (Gn 1:1-2).

God the Father utters His creative Word by calling His Spirit down upon the cosmos in a continuous cosmic *epiclesis* (in Greek, a calling down upon) to divinize matter into spirit. God breathes His breath, his *ruah*, His loving Spirit, as the principle of life into all His creation. The beasts of the land are sustained by His *ruah*. The heavens are also the work of God's enspiriting breath, His Spirit (Gn 7:15).

But in a special way God breathes His breath into man and woman and they become human persons (*nephesh* in Hebrew), capable of communicating with God who makes them destined to share in His very own image and likeness (Gn 1:26-27). But all human beings, by the inbreathing of God's Spirit, are called also to cooperate in harmonizing all of creation into a work of conscious love, a harmony of diversity in oneness through love (Gn 1:28-30).

Of all material creatures, only man and woman have free will to respond through personal choices to God's call to share in His intimate community of love through His Spirit. The necessity for decision, an obligation which we can never evade, is the distinguishing feature of us human beings. "It is the being created by God to stand 'over-against' Him, to reply to God, and in this answer alone to fulfill — or destroy — the purpose of God's creation."[3]

A LOVE COVENANT

If God's Spirit is operating throughout all of nature, fashioning woman, man and all other creatures in a mysterious awesome way, His Spirit is more powerfully operating in His merciful, *hesed* covenantal love for His chosen people. God's Spirit comes upon individuals and His entire people to restore them to new love relationships with Him. God is most loving Spirit when He is renewing His people by giving them a new heart. "I shall give you a new heart, and put a new spirit in you" (Ezk 36:26).

God breathes His love. Repentance allows His people and individuals to open up to receive His breathing-in-Spirit of love to become quickened again, to share life-giving relationships with Yahweh. We have been made for communion, a "union with" God and fellow human beings and in union with the entire material world around us. God is love and we, through His abiding, loving presence dwelling within us, are to receive His loving energies and thus live in communion through His Spirit of love with all persons we meet. We begin to move toward loving communion by means of "communication."

But communication is only the first step in becoming "present" to another. In language we relay information to another on a linear level. This information tends to be logical: facts, ideas that are comprehensible to our human reasoning, as in science. We can also learn certain facts about God given to us through revelation in Scripture and in oral traditions.

But there is a higher level of knowledge. This is communion between friends and lovers, between ourselves and our loving God.

This communion is effected through the operations of the Holy
Spirit.

> *The hidden wisdom of God which we teach in our mysteries is the*
> *wisdom that God predestined to be for our glory before the ages*
> *began. . . . These are the very things that God has revealed to us*
> *through the Spirit, for the Spirit reaches the depths of everything,*
> *even the depths of God. . . . Now instead of the Spirit of the world,*
> *we have received the Spirit that comes from God, to teach us to*
> *understand the gifts that he has given us. . . . (1 Cor 2:7-13).*

THE SPIRIT AS A PRESENCE OF LOVE

God becomes actively present to us and invites us into intimate union with Him through His Spirit of love. It is only God's
love, His Spirit, who can bring about true communion in love.
When God created woman and gave her to man, He breathed His
created Spirit of intimate love into them and bound them together
into a union, bone from his bone and flesh from his flesh (Gn 2:23).
God joined them together in love and they became "one body"
(Gn 2:24) and no force in the world was to cut this union asunder.
Christianity would guarantee that whenever we live in love toward
each other, it is the Holy Spirit who is perfecting the love of God on
earth, enfleshing it in a new incarnation in the material world (1 Jn
4:12).

In loving another, we become a gifted presence of God's
Spirit of love to that person. We wish to live in union (the true
meaning of "communion") with that person so as to be present as
often as possible, not only physically in space and time, but more
importantly in the inner recesses of our consciousness. We become
present to each other in deeper and deeper consciousness to the
degree that we can share our most intimate thoughts through
speech. We need words, such as "I love you," not to give new,

logical information, but to launch a deeper moving into communion with another. Without internal words that can be expressed in externalized words, spoken or written or acted out in gestures, we would never grow in love.

But we are this way because God is this way in His nature as love. God the Father in absolute silence, in a communication of love impossible for us human beings to understand, speaks His one eternal Word through His Spirit of love. In that one Word, the Father is perfectly present, totally self-giving to His Son. But in His Spirit, the Father also hears His Word come back to Him in a perfect, eternal "yes" of total surrendering love, that is again the Holy Spirit.

The Trinity is the reciprocal community of a movement of the Spirit of love between Father and Son through the Holy Spirit. God becomes real as He communicates in love with His Word. His Word gives Him His identity as Father. But that means eternal self-giving to the Other, His Word in love, the Holy Spirit.

THE WORD REVEALS THE SPIRIT OF LOVE

From the revealed word of God in the Old and New Testaments and in the living tradition of the Church through the centuries, the divine nature is considered as totally transcendent and inaccessible, uncommunicable to us (Ex 3:4 ff; Is 6.) Yet Jesus Christ promises us that this inaccessible God with the life of the Trinity will descend and enter into our very beings and abide immanently within us. "If anyone loves me he will keep my word and my Father will love him, and we shall come to him and make our home with him" (Jn 14:23).

Jesus Christ is the Word and the Son of the Father, the Way, the Truth and the Life, who brings us into the awesome mystery of the Trinity as a communion in its own life through His revealing Holy Spirit. From this revelation of the Holy Spirit we can believe that the Father begets eternally His only Begotten Son through His Spirit of love. Since the Son is one in substance with the Father, He, through the incarnation, can bring us, not only to a knowledge of the Father, but He can actualize us through His Holy Spirit to be children of God, sharing in His very own nature (2 P 1:4). "God became man in order that man could become God" was the constant teaching of the early Fathers, taken from St. Irenaeus.

REGENERATED AS CHILDREN OF GOD THROUGH THE SPIRIT

The Spirit, that the risen Jesus sends by asking His Father, is seen as the loving force of God Himself, divinizing all who are open to receive His Gift of the Spirit. This holiness given to us to transform us into heirs of God, true children of God (Rm 8:15), is the very indwelling of God's Spirit taking possession of us Christians, penetrating our minds, our thoughts, and all our actions with the very life of God.

St. John, the beloved Disciple of Jesus, cannot get over the miracle of our regeneration, ". . . not by water alone but by the Spirit. . . ." (Jn 3:3, 5). "Think of the love that the Father has lavished on us, by letting us be called God's children; and that is what we are" (1 Jn 3:1). St. Paul describes the main work of the Spirit as making us into true children of God: ". . . the Spirit of God has made his home in you . . . and if the Spirit of him who raised Jesus from the dead is living in you, then he who raised Jesus from the dead will give life to your own mortal bodies through his Spirit living in you" (Rm 8:9, 11).

God's very own Spirit dwells within us as in His temple (1 Cor 6:19-20). We possess through the Spirit the fullness of the triune God living and acting in love within us at all times. This Spirit of love brings new life to its fullness in the proportion that we allow the Spirit to become our Guide, Teacher and Revealer, as

He guides us Christians to make choices according to the mind of Christ.

STIFLING THE HOLY SPIRIT

The work of God's Spirit is to heal, integrate and transform all the hidden potentialities lying within our consciousness and unconscious. Yet the majority of human beings, including the greater number of Christians, live unaware of the creative, transforming presence in their lives of the Holy Spirit and their possibility of bringing that Spirit into the world through creative work in the Spirit of love.

This gentle breeze is capable of changing itself into a storm. This watchful flame can ignite into a raging incendiary of loving fire to bring about world peace and justice. This Spirit is in every human being because God Trinity is love, actively involved in every aspect of his/her life. The Spirit's work is to form each person toward the good, the best in her/himself, for the truth, for love, opening human eyes to recognize and love Christ, awakening one's dormant faith and fortifying and guiding each person. The Holy Spirit is the great builder of unity by being the internal, personalized force of self-emptying love which acts as a path and which pulsates, pushes toward maturation, guides toward convergence and unifies all that has been dispersed.

Most of us are not free. We are held captive by our dark side, our false *ego*. We live in a constant fear of life and of death. By refusing to live at the center of our spirit-to-God's Spirit level, we are barraged constantly by fearful thoughts of our unworthiness, of sin and death. We are not integrated, whole and holy people. We are convinced that we are ugly and that no one truly loves us!

The time comes when we are tired with the low-level of living and accepting the brokenness that has produced the person we may be at this given time. Then we can rise with a burst of Spirit-filled will-determination on our part and say with the prodigal son: ''Yes, I shall arise and go home to my father!'' Only then can we enjoy true freedom that consists in a passing-over from a state of disintegration to a condition of completeness, from impersonality to personality, from passivity to creativeness. In a word, true freedom and holiness consists in our integrating all levels of our being under the dynamic action of God's love, that in Scripture is called the Spirit of God.

OUR SPIRIT AND GOD'S SPIRIT

St. Paul describes our integration as the bringing of *spirit, soul* and *body* into perfection or holiness:

May the God of peace make you perfect and holy; and may you all be kept safe and blameless, spirit, soul and body, for the coming of our Lord Jesus Christ (1 Th 5:23).

How are we, as human beings, to relate directly with God's Spirit? We can easily understand, even in the language of the simplest people, that we are made up of body and soul. To understand the concept of our human *spirit* concretely, beyond any poetic use to refer to our soul-faculties, we need prayerfully to reflect on Holy Scripture. There we will discover that the human spirit cannot be considered as a static part of a human being's makeup.

The human spirit in Scripture is seen as the human person viewed in his/her unique personality through a knowing relationship in love toward God. It is the total human being responding to God's personal call to enter into an intimate love relationship through God's Spirit of love. We can better understand what our human spirit means by studying the teachings of the early Eastern Fathers who built a theological anthropology around the biblical model of image and likeness.[4] Simply put in the teachings of St. Irenaeus of the 2nd century, we are made by God "according to the image of God," who is Jesus Christ. We are not the image of God; only the Word made flesh is (Col 1:15). But all human beings are created in a dynamic relationship of moving the basic "image-ness" relationship to that of ever more conscious loving oneness in the "likeness" of Christ.

All human beings are born and progress from early childhood into ever more developed relationships on the body and soul levels. We are a psycho-physical unity, a personality in relation to the created material world around us. This is not a person with a body, but an *embodied* being in inter-relations with the created world around him/herself. As an *ensouled* being, we also have soul-relations through the psyche with all the emotions and passions along with the intellectual and volitional life that allow us to relate to other "souled-beings."

IN THE LIKENESS TO CHRIST

But we are not born, like the caterpillar, having the wings of the spirit by which we can relate intimately and personally with God through His Spirit of love. The potential is locked inside of all body and soul relations. The *likeness* to Jesus Christ has not evolved yet. This is possible only through the release of the Holy Spirit within us. We come into spirit-relationships through a knowing relationship in love with God. It is an awakening through God's Spirit, directly intervening by His infusion of faith, hope and love into our entire being. It is God, Trinity, as Grace, uncreated energies of love, calling us to receive the Gift of Himself of the Spirit of love. The Spirit sets up as almost an embryonic life of God living within us through created, sanctifying grace, that can increase and diminish all through our earthly lives as we freely opt to

surrender to the transforming power of the Spirit into a greater
oneness with the indwelling Word made flesh, Jesus Christ.
St. Irenaeus offers us his succinct teaching in this statement:

> *But when the spirit here blended with the soul is united to God's
> handiwork, the man is rendered spiritual and perfect because of
> the outpouring of the Spirit, and this is he who was made in the
> image and likeness of God. But if the Spirit be wanting to the
> soul, he who is such is indeed of an animal nature, and being left
> carnal, shall be an imperfect being, possessing indeed the image
> of God in his formation, but not receiving the likeness through the
> Spirit and thus in this being imperfect. . . . Those then are the
> perfect who have had the Spirit of God remaining in them, and
> have preserved their souls and bodies blameless, holding fast the
> faith of God, that is, that faith which is directed towards God and
> maintaining righteous dealings with respect to their neighbors.* [5]

The paradox of birth to new levels of conscious integration
through transcendent love demands a preceding death to all that
inhibits this growth of our spirit under the guidance of God's Spirit.
The first experience of the Spirit is like an outpouring from the
transcendent invisible, incomprehensible presence of the Trinity as
a mighty wind, a frenzied fire of God's love, the Spirit. It is as if the
Spirit descends upon every person who in a crisis of choices
struggles to choose what his/her conscience presents as the morally
better choice. This may come through natural calamities of earth-
quakes, famine, impending death or grave sickness, in time of war
or bereavement. The Holy Spirit has always been present operating
as God's personalized love in all bodied and souled experiences,
humbly knocking at our heart's door to effect our spirit-to-God's
Spirit relationship. We are called to wake up from our sleep to
accept His new "coming" to us through His constant outpouring
gifts of faith, hope and love.

Yet we are never forced by the Spirit to yield to His transforming presence. The gate that leads to this new love consciousness is

small and the road narrow (Mt 7:14). We could say the Spirit calls all human beings since God effectively desires that all persons attain the goal for which He has created them, to enjoy His divine life eternally. The Spirit respects our free will. Yet the Spirit also pushes us to a conversion by demanding of us an upheaval of all our values that have come to us as we lived not yet on the spirit level.

ENTERING INTO THE BARREN DESERT

The Spirit is always operating actively to bring us into the constant love of God, abiding within us. But that we might be open to the power of the Spirit, we need to be cleansed of all self-centered narcissism or pride. The Spirit is not a magician, but love that invites us to become involved in the process of integration. This is the call of the Spirit that we enter into the inner desert of our hearts where we can and must face and accept our brokenness and in joyous faith trust in the Spirit's help that we can live in goodness.

We must confront the dark, shadow side of our inner psyche over which the Spirit of God's love continues to hover to bring forth new life out of what seems to be only death. The Spirit brings about a healing integration that is a slow process demanding constancy and patience on our part as we cooperate with the purifying Spirit. Prerequisite for healing through the Spirit is a childlike trust in accepting sincerely where we are at in the present now-moment. Whatever we fail to face and acknowledge as a part of us cannot be healed and transformed. Humility comes through our wrestling like Jacob with God in our brokenness in the darkness of our psyche.

In the desert of our hearts we enter into a silence that becomes a spiritual poverty. This is the result of experiencing the infinite riches of God's love for us as the Father begets within our heart the very presence of His Word made flesh, Jesus Christ, through the loving Spirit. It is an entering into a state of true knowledge of ourselves and of God, that is sheer gift of the Holy Spirit. It is the purity of heart that Jesus promised to give us as true vision to see God everywhere.

As we move away from our false ego as an independent unit, living in self-absorption, our true ego or self as a unique, autonomous person, acting through the Spirit in humble obedience to Christ, gains new consciousness. We surrender all God's endowments given to us in our creation and in our willed development and place them under the guidance of the Spirit of love. We allow the Spirit to use these gifts as charisms in service to others, so they may also attain their uniqueness as we strive to build a better world of peace and justice for all of God's children.

THE SPIRIT WORKING THROUGHOUT THE ENTIRE WORLD

The true test that we are being guided by the Spirit's power of godly love always lies in our changed attitude toward other human beings and the entire world around us. Dr. Karlfried Graf Durckheim describes this new consciousness:

> . . . *freed from his small ego — released from pride, from the desire to dominate, the fear of pain, the longing for security — he becomes firmly anchored in his true center. Thus centered, he is able to be receptive to the forces of Being which, with or without his awareness, transform, support, shape and protect him to reveal these forces to the world by the quality of his work, his ability to create and his capacity for love.* [6]

The true sign that individuals and corporate religions are moving under the guidance of the Spirit is found in all our social relationships of oneness with the Spirit, who alone creates unity in diversity. Love alone counts and it alone can overcome the powers of evil. Such love is God's creative, transforming power of the Spirit operating in the individual person and a community of like-loving persons.

The Spirit of love cannot be limited exclusively to any human myopic views of what constitutes truth. That there are different paths to God as witnessed by the many religions that are given throughout the world to so many millions and millions, other than Christians, is quite evident. That good and sanctifying lives come out of such religions is proved by the fruit produced by the individuals who sincerely with discipline follow such paths.

Fr. Karl Rahner points out to us: "The world is drawn to its spiritual fulfillment by the Spirit of God, who directs that whole history of the world in all its length and breadth towards its proper goal."[7]

Jesus Himself promises that we all can receive the guidance of the Holy Spirit: "Ask, and it will be given to you; search, and you will find, knock, and the door will be opened to you. For the one who asks always receives; the one who searches always finds; the one who knocks will always have the door opened to him. . . . If you then, who are evil, know how to give your children what is good, how much more will the heavenly Father give the Holy Spirit to those who ask him!" (Lk 11:9-13).

SALVATION OPENED TO ALL

Vatican II affirms this belief that the Spirit operates in a salvific way by imparting grace to all who seek salvation: "Those also can attain to everlasting salvation who . . . sincerely seek God and moved by grace, strive by their deeds to do His will."[8] This does not infer any sense of religious indifferentism. All religions are not of equal value in bringing individuals to the fullness of God's revelation.

Dr. Charles DeCelles in his book, *The Unbound Spirit*, makes an important distinction:

> *There is no question of religious indifferentism here. Rather an implicit recognition of the unbound nature of the Spirit, who works wherever he chooses. Ramakrishna is wrong when he opines that climate, temperament and name alone explain the differences in the religions of the world. But he is on the right track when he suggests that those who kneel in sincere adoration worship the one God, and that he reveals himself to them in a meaningful and salvific way. For God indeed "enlightens all men so that they may finally have life."*[9]

If there is one supreme God whose nature remains always incomprehensible to us, yet this God is always good, loving and merciful in His active concern for all His children. We must believe He is always working actively that all will effectively have all the means to attain that predestined goal God had for each human being from all eternity. Therefore, we must hold that God's Holy Spirit is available to all men and women. Through the Spirit, therefore, all human beings can obtain salvation.

This accepted teaching among all Catholic theologians today is well expressed by P.C. Mozoomdar:

> *All men see the Spirit, most men ignore him, exceedingly few realize him. . . . That amid the chances, changes, and delusions of life, this one Reality, may cast his unfailing radiance in all dark places, and make myriad manifestations of himself that we may hold by him, dwell in him, know, love, and trust him at all times with the certainty and security we long for, faithful men in every age have spoken to us their experiences. These experiences are so simple and natural that under certain conditions of mental awakening they exact universal response. . . . Whatever ultimate mysteries there may be in the great depths of the External Being,*

*there is no expression that makes such a direct appeal to the
restless instincts of our nature as that God is, that he is near, that
he is in the heart, and that he is great and good, and we had better
fly to him as to our refuge and home.* [10]

A WIDENING CONCEPT OF CHURCH

Thus with the bishops of Vatican II, we can and must broaden
our concept of Church to-embrace the whole of humanity. "This
Second Vatican Council, having probed more profoundly into the
mystery of the Church, now addresses itself without hesitation . . .
to the whole of humanity." [11] The active presence of the Holy
Spirit is found wherever a person lives in agapic love, that is,
self-emptying love on behalf of the well-being of another. Simply
put, we can say that, where love is, God is also, as we find
expressed in 1 Jn 4:16.

We see this in the lives of holy men and women in all the great
and noble non-Christian religions as well as among the Christian
saints. Today the Spirit has opened Westerners to find the beautiful
and the good in all cultures and in all peoples, but also in all
religions. It becomes easier in personal dialogue with members of
such religions and through reading their religious classics in trans-
lations than in times past for us Christians to discover there the
working of the sanctifying Spirit.

A concrete example of a Spirit-filled Hindu is Mohandas
Gandhi (1869-1948), father of independent India. The American
bishops held Gandhi up as a model of ethical behavior through his
very Christian living out the nonviolence of Jesus. [12] Thomas
Merton with great conviction holds Gandhi up for all Christians to
imitate his courage to follow God's voice.

*A Christian can do nothing greater than follow his own con-
science with a fidelity comparable to that which Gandhi obeyed*

what he believed to be the voice of God. Gandhi is, it seems to me,
a model of integrity whom we cannot afford to ignore, and the one
basic duty we all owe to the world of our time is to imitate him in
"disassociating ourselves from evil in total disregard of the
consequences."[13]

NEW AND EXCITING CHALLENGES

As we move into the 21st century, we find ourselves entering into new and exciting challenges of cosmic dimensions. We find ourselves being enriched as we dialogue with others of all other religions in our common spiritual quests. But we also find ourselves opening up to the same unifying Spirit who moves us or at least invites us powerfully to join with all humanity to face together the cosmic problems that threaten all of us in our future survival.

But before we can reach a Christic consciousness of oneness with other human beings outside of ourselves and create a oneness-community on a cosmic, global level, we must become transformed by the Holy Spirit into individual persons who realize they are free because they have experienced God's personalized love for us. Only a healed and loving person, one with God's community of love, can have the freedom to give his or her life in loving service to others. This experiential knowledge of our new selves in Christ through the revelation of the Spirit takes place primarily in deep, interior prayer.

ABANDONMENT IN CONTEMPLATION

It is, therefore, inwardly that we are to go to find our true freedom. The Spirit leads us into a process of our letting go of the controlled activity we have been exercising in our habitual, prayer-encounters with the indwelling Trinity. As the Holy Spirit infuses the gifts of deep faith, hope and love into our hearts, we are able to surrender to the indwelling presence of the risen Lord Jesus.

Our aggressive activity both in prayer and in our daily actions takes on a gentleness and docility to the inner world and loving activities of God's indwelling presence within and without throughout the world. There is a "letting go" of our own separated power from the Ultimate Source of all power and a new sensitivity, a new listening to God's presence and loving activity around us takes over. We begin to live on a new plateau of conscious awareness of God's active, energizing presence in each moment. Whether there is ardent consolation or arid dryness, there seems to be a continued state of deep peace and joy that no event or person can take from us.

The whole world now becomes a diaphanous presence of God's love, shining through to you. No longer do you find a world that is somehow sacred and a different world that is profane and lost to God's presence. You see now the world in all its uniqueness and yet precisely that uniqueness is discovered in the finality of God's created love.

The Spirit gifts you with an intuitive knowledge by which you discover God at the core of each person you encounter. A reverence sweeps over you as you open to God in each human being, as you abandon yourself to serve that godly presence and work with that loving activity of God's Spirit.

REINTEGRATION

You begin to return to your true state, to a consciousness of being *in Christ.* "And for anyone who is in Christ, there is a new creation; the old creation has gone, and now the new one is here. It is all God's work" (2 Cor 5:17). This contemplative prayer is the fruit of the Holy Spirit, yet demands our own cooperation. It differs from any transcendental meditation techniques or occult practices to attain a oneness experience with the Absolute. Such other techniques focus on the human efforts alone to reach perfection, excluding the personalized gifting of God Trinity through the free activities of the Holy Spirit.

This is a dynamic process of continued purification and dying to selfishness and a rising to a more intense conscious relationship to God. As God reveals Himself to you through a faith that grows ever deeper, your interior powers expand and stretch forth toward God as your only desire. You are filled with an increase of God's uncreated energies, that assimilate you into a great unity with the triune community of Father, Son and Holy Spirit. There is peace and joy in the transforming union already experienced. There is a burning desire still more to possess the seeming "absent" God by a stretching out in a willed-desire to surrender oneself more completely, to suffer even more for love of God.

MOVING TO BUILD A BETTER WORLD

You enter into a personal transformation of yourself into a union with Christ through His Spirit. You experience that out of your brokenness and sinfulness you have become transformed into a divinized child of God, loved infinitely by the Trinity unto the death of Jesus poured out to image that constant triune love within you. You are personally transformed into Christ and yet also into uniqueness, different and distinct, but now seemingly never separable from Him. You begin to believe and hope in the same Jesus of glory as an active leaven inserted into the mass of creation and raising the whole created world through His transforming, creative Holy Spirit, into the fullness destined for it by the Father. The whole of creation is now like a pregnant mother in agony before giving birth, groaning and laboring in pain until the new life of a new creation comes forth (Rm 8:22).

You yield to Christ's reconciling power to be used as an instrument to make all things new through His Spirit. He is "the First-born from the dead, the Ruler of the kings of the earth. He loves us and has washed away our sins with his blood, and made us a line of kings, priests to serve His God and Father" (Rv 1:5-6).

You enter into a solidarity with the saints and angels, with the living members of the Body of Christ, the Church. You are also one with the suffering world, with those who lie in ignorance and darkness of their own uniqueness in Christ. You burn actively to bring them into the light. You are humble and want to wash the feet of your brothers and sisters, since you have experienced your great dignity in the humility of Jesus Christ, who emptied Himself, becoming obedient unto death for love of you (Ph 2:10).

HE EMPTIED HIMSELF

Such a contemplative looks down into God's incompleted world, the world that He is still creating with our human cooperation. The person of prayer is much like Mary, the Mother of God, as she entered into the cave of Bethlehem. It surely was not the idealized cave of Italian religious art or popular Christmas cards. Mary brought forth Jesus and laid Him in a manger of straw.

This was the real world into which God was entering to begin His transfiguring process. It was His world, real and unfinished, which he saw as "very good" (Gn 1:31). Christ as a newly born child was stripped of everything as a sign of what was to come. He was the mustard seed, so insignificant, yet from it would come the huge tree that would harbor the birds of the air. The process of re-creation was beginning. The evolution of the People of God and the transfiguration of the universe by Christ's taboric lights was beginning with this *Proton* of Divine Love.

Here we encounter the simplicity, the monad of divinity beginning with a spark of humanity. Nothing else. Mary and

Joseph meet "raw" nature. Nothing of the technical world around. From such a simple, ordinary beginning, God would manifest His great love for us. God calls us downward to enter into His suffering world. Once we experience through the overshadowing of the Holy Spirit in prayer the transfiguring power of God's love for us, we can love His world by surrendering ourselves to His presence. We do this in order to serve and to bring Him forth more radiantly and more explicitly, so that the whole world may recognize that He is the Source of all being. In discovering God at our center, we discover Him also as the center of His world. Rooted in God, we can go forth and love the world as God loves it. We move at each moment from light to greater light, from God to God in all things.

Heaven has begun even on this earth. We have died to self and already have risen with Christ. We have put on the thoughts of things above, because we have now already begun to glimpse the reality that, as St. Paul says, Jesus Christ is in all things (Col 3:11). The Heavenly Jerusalem is now piercing through the suffering shadows of a world that is still groaning before it is brought into the full life already glimpsed as present.

AN INVOLVING LOVE

The true test of how Christian we are and to what degree we have been baptized in the Holy Spirit is the degree of our involvement in bringing mercy and love to those suffering. "For I was hungry and you gave me food. . . ." (Mt 25:35-40). We as Christians need to hear the anguished cry for justice and human dignity rising from our suffering brothers and sisters and make their burdens and sufferings our own since Christ has already entered into a oneness with their sufferings. What affects others must affect us deeply, since, when one person suffers, Christ and all of us suffer.

The presence of God within you becomes a swelling ocean wave that seeks to burst through the space of your heart to flow out and inundate the entire world before you with God's love. You whisper the name and presence of Father, Son and Holy Spirit over your world. What was hidden now becomes revealed, what was absent now through your cooperation becomes present. As the Holy Spirit broods over you, baptizing you with His love and fire, you are able to be a transfigured microcosmos that can re-incarnate Jesus Christ, the God-Man. You manifest in place and time the Son of the Father whose Spirit of love overshadows the not-yetness of this cosmos, the macrocosmos that is to become the Heavenly Jerusalem.

A most fitting close to this book is Gerard Manley Hopkins' beautiful poem:

GOD'S GRANDEUR

The world is charged with the
grandeur of God.
It will flame out, like shining
from shook foil;
It gathers to a greatness, like
the ooze of oil;
Crushed. Why do men then now not
reck his rod?
Generations have trod, have trod,
have trod;
And all is seared with trade;
bleared, smeared with toil;
And wears man's smudge and shares
man's smell: the soil
Is bare now, nor can foot feel,
being shod.

*And for all this, nature is never
spent;*
    *There lives the dearest freshness
deep down things;*
    *And though the last lights off the
black West went*
    *Oh, morning, at the brown brink
eastward, spring —*
    *Because the Holy Ghost over the
bent*
    *World broods with warm breast and
with ah! bright wings.* [14]

ENDNOTES

Chapter One: *The Beginnings of a New Age*

1 Lewis Mumford: *The Transfiguration of Man* (N.Y.: Harper Bros., 1956), p. 231.
2 Marilyn Ferguson: *The Aquarian Conspiracy* (Los Angeles: J.P. Tarcher Inc., 1980), pp. 23-24.
3 *Time*: "New Age Harmonies" (Dec. 7, 1987), pp. 62, 64.
4 Representative of such fundamentalistic books that usually defend Christianity against the "Satanism" of the New Age movement are: Dave Hunt & T.A. McMahon: *America: The Sorcerer's New Apprentice: The Rise of New Age Shamanism; The Seduction of Christianity: Spiritual Discernment in the Last Days* (Eugene, OR: Harvest House Publishers, 1988 and 1987 respectively); Constance Cumbey: *The Hidden Dangers of the Rainbow: The New Age Movement and Our Coming Age of Barbarism* (Shreveport, LA: Huntington House, Inc., 1983); William Kirk Kilpatrick: *Psychological Seduction* (Nashville, TN: T. Nelson, 1983).
5 Thomas Kuhn: *The Structure of Scientific Revolutions* (Chicago, IL: University of Chicago Press, 1970, 2nd edition).
6 Norman Pittenger: *Process Thought & Christian Faith* (N.Y.: Macmillan, 1968), p. 13.
7 Willis Harman: *Global Mind Change* (Indianapolis, IN: Knowledge Systems Inc., 1988), pp. 34-35.
8 Ibid., pp. 38-39.
9 Ibid., p. 39.
10 Fritjof Capra: *The Tao of Physics* (Berkeley, CA: Shambhala, 1975) p. 138.
11 Quoted by Lincoln Barnett: *The Universe and Dr. Einstein* (N.Y.: New American Library, 1962), p. 108.
12 F. Capra, op. cit., Ch. 10 endnote 2, quotes Ashvaghosha: *The Awakening of Faith*; tr. by D.T. Suzuki (Chicago: Open Court, 1900), p. 55.

Chapter Two: *Developing an Earth Spirituality*

1 Joan Didion: *The White Album* (N.Y.: Simon & Schuster, 1979), p. 11.
2 Cf.: Patricia Mische: "Toward a Global Spirituality," pp. 4-14, in: *The Whole Earth Papers*, no. 16, 1982 (Global Education Assoc.: E. Orange, NJ).
3 Ibid., p. 5.
4 V.E. Frankl: *La psychothérapie et son image de l'homme* (Paris, 1970), p. 150.

5 Ibid., p. 152.

6 St. Thomas Aquinas: *Summa Theologiae*: Prima Pars, 13, 7 ad 4.

7 Louis Dupré: "Transcendence & Immanence as Theological Categories," in: *Proceedings of the 31st Annual Convention of the Catholic Theological Society of America*, 31 (1976), pp. 1-10.

8 Lynn White Jr.: "The Historical Roots of Our Ecologic Crisis," in: *The Subversive Science: Essays Toward an Ecology of Man*; eds. Paul Shepard and Dan McKinley (Boston, 1969), pp. 350-351. This essay originally appeared in *Science*, 155, 1967, pp. 1203-1207.

9 See H. Paul Santmire: *Brother Earth: Nature, God and Ecology in a Time of Crisis* (N.Y.: Thomas Nelson, 1970), esp. Ch. IV. Also his article: "Reflections on the Alleged Ecological Bankruptcy of Western Theology," in: *Ethics for Environment: Three Religious Strategies* (The Proceedings of a National Conference held at the University of Wisconsin-Green Bay, June 11-13, 1973) (UWGB Ecumenical Center, 1973), pp. 23-46.

10 Edwin A. Burtt: *The Metaphysical Foundations of Modern Physical Science*, revised ed. (London: Kegan, Paul, Trubner, 1932), p. 236f.

11 I. Kant: *Critique of Teleological Judgment*, tr. J.C. Meredith (Oxford: Clarendon Press, 1928), p. 394.

12 Lewis Mumford: *Technics and Civilization* (N.Y.: Harcourt, Brace, 1934), p. 25.

13. Cf.: George A. Maloney, S.J.: "The Role of Values and Ethics in Environmental Concerns," in: *Ethics for Environment: Three Religious Strategies*, op. cit., p. 9.

14 *The New York Times*, Nov. 1, 1970.

15 Thomas Berry: *The Dream of the Earth* (San Francisco: Sierra Club Books, 1988), p. 200.

16 An unpublished translation from the original Sanscrit by Michael Meehan, S.J.

17 Teilhard de Chardin: *The Divine Milieu*; tr. B. Wall (London: Wm. Collins Sons & Co., 1960), pp. 76-78.

18 Thomas Merton: *Conjectures of a Guilty Bystander* (Garden City, N.Y.: Doubleday, 1965), pp. 141-142.

19 The full text of Chief Seattle's speech in 1854 when his tribe was asked to sell tribal lands to the U.S. Government can be found in: *Power to the People: Active Nonviolence in the US* (Culver City, CA: Peace Press, 1977). Quote cited by P. Mische, art. cit., p. 9.

20 Quoted by P. Mische in art. cit., p. 11.

21 Cf. Donald P. Gray: *A New Creation Story* (Chambersburg, PA: Anima Books, 1979) pp. 5-6.

22 See the treatment of these phrases of Teilhard's thinking of world evolution in: George Maloney, S.J.: *The Cosmic Christ: From Paul to Teilhard* (N.Y.: Sheed & Ward, 1968), pp. 194-220.

23 Cf. Donald P. Gray, op. cit., p. 6.

24 Teilhard de Chardin: *Christianity & Evolution* (N.Y.: Harcourt, Bruce, Jovanovich, 1974), pp. 92-93.

Chapter Three: *A Logos Mysticism*

1 Karl Jaspers: *The Origin & Goal of History* (New Haven: Yale University Press, 1953).

2 Ewert Cousins: "Teilhard & Global Spirituality," in: *Anima*, Fall, 1981, p. 28. Cf. also: Wm. M. Thompson: *Christ and Consciousness* (N.Y./Ramsey: Paulist Press, 1977), pp. 20-23.

3 Op. cit., p. 21.

4 John B. Cobb: *The Structure of Christian Existence* (Philadelphia: Westminster Press, 1967), pp. 52-59.

5 Cf.: Serge Bulgakov: "De Verbe Incarné," in: *La Sagesse Divine et la Théanthropie* (Paris: Aubier, 1943), pp. 65-68; also G. Maloney, S.J.: *Man the Divine Icon* (Pecos, NM: Dove, 1973).

6 Emil Brunner: *Man in Revolt* (London: Lutterworth Press, 1939), pp. 97-98.

7 Cf.: Otto Procksch's article: "Logos," in *Theological Dictionary of the New Testament*; ed. Gerhard Kittel and tr. by Geoffrey W. Bromiley (Grand Rapids, MI: Wm. B. Eerdmans Publishing Co., 1967), p. 92.

8 R. Bultmann: *Theology of the New Testament*, tr. by Kendrick Grobel; Vol. 2 (N.Y.: Charles Scribner's Sons, 1955), pp. 60-61; 63.

9 Cf. Vladimir Lossky: *The Mystical Theology of the Eastern Church* (London: Wm. Collins & Sons & Co., 1968), p. 98.

10 Polycarp Sherwood, O.S.B.: *The Earlier Ambigua of St. Maximus the Confessor* (Rome: San Anselmo Press, 1955), p. 176.

11 G.M. Hopkins: "Hurrahing in Harvest," in: *A Hopkins Reader*, ed. John Peck (N.Y./London: Oxford University Press, 1953), p. 15.

12 Thomas Merton: *Seeds of Contemplation* (Norfolk: Dell Books, 1949), p. 59.

Chapter Four: *Resurrection and a New Creation*

1 Alexander Solzhenitsyn: *The Gulag Archipelago, 1918-1956: An Experiment in Literary Investigation*; Vol. 2, tr. Thomas P. Whitney (N.Y.: Harper & Row, 1975), p. 615.

2 Walther Eichrodt: *Man in the Old Testament* (London: Allenson, 1966), p. 21.

3 Ibid., p. 23.

4 Eric Voegelin: *Order & History* (Baton Rouge: Louisiana State University Press, 1956-1974), Vol. 1, p. 484.

5 John Cobb: *The Structure of Christian Existence* (Philadelphia: Westminster Press, 1967), p. 109.

6 A.M. Ramsey: *The Resurrection of Christ* (London: G. Bless, 1945), p. 31.

7 F.X. Durrwell: *The Resurrection: A Biblical Study*; 2nd ed., tr. Rosemary Sheed (N.Y.: Sheed & Ward, 1960), p. 32.

8 Cf. George A. Maloney, S.J.: *The First Day of Eternity: Resurrection Now* (N.Y.: Crossroad, 1982), where I have further developed this concept.

9 Durrwell: op. cit., p. 8.

10 P.C. Hodgson: *Jesus: Word and Presence* (Philadelphia: Fortress Press, 1971), pp. 220-291.

11 Peter DeRosa: *Come, Holy Spirit* (Milwaukee: Bruce Co., 1968), p. 60.

Chapter Five: *The Christic Universe*

1 Pierre Teilhard de Chardin: *The Divine Milieu*, tr. B. Wall (London: Wm. Collins Sons & Co., 1960), p. 14.

2 H. Schlier: "Anakephaloioomai," in: *Theologische Worterbuch*, III (Stuttgart: W. Kohlhammer, 1938), pp. 681 ff.

3 J. Huby: *Les Épîtres de la Captivitaté* (Paris: Beauchesnes, 1935), p. 40.

4 G.A. Maloney, S.J.: *The Cosmic Christ: From Paul to Teilhard* (N.Y.: Sheed & Ward, 1968).

5 R.C. Zaehner: "Teilhard and Eastern Religions," in: *The Teilhard Review*, 2 (Winter, 1967-8), pp. 41 ff.

6 Henri de Lubac: *the Religion of Teilhard de Chardin*; tr. René Hague (N.Y.: Desclée, 1967), pp. 88 ff.

7 Teilhard de Chardin: *The Phenomenon of Man*; tr. Bernard Wall (London: Wm. Collins Sons & Co., 1959), pp. 56-57.

8 Teilhard de Chardin: *Écrits du temps de la guerre, 1916-1919* (Paris: Grasset, 1965), p. 5. English translation: *Writings in Time of War* (N.Y.: Harper & Row, 1968), p. 14.

9 Teilhard: *Les noms de la Matierre*, 1919, in: *Ecrits*, p. 425. This essay is not included in the English translation.

10 Teilhard: *Réflexions sur la probabilité scientifique*, 1951, in: *L'Activation de l'énergie* (Paris: Editions du Seul, 1963), p. 282.

11 *The Phenomenon of Man*, op. cit., p. 244.

12 Ibid., p. 297.

13 Teilhard: *The Future of Man*, tr. N. Denny (N.Y.: Harper & Row, 1964), pp. 82-89.

14 Teilhard: *Comment Je Vois* (1948); unpublished.

15 Teilhard: *La Vie Cosmique* (1916) in: *Ecrits* . . . op. cit., pp. 39-40, 47.

16 Teilhard: *Mon Universe*; cited by H. de Lubac, op. cit., p. 123.

17 Cited by Mary Evelyn Tucker: *The Ecological Spirituality of Teilhard; Teilhard Studies*, no. 13 (Spring, 1985) (Chambersburg, PA: Anima Books, 1985), p. 11.

18 Much of what is contained in this chapter can be found in greater development in my book: *The Cosmic Christ: From Paul to Teilhard* (N.Y.: Sheed & Ward, 1968), pp. 182-220. Some leading works on Teilhard's ideas are the following: Neville Braybrooke, ed.; *Teilhard de Chardin: Pilgrim of the Future* (N.Y.: Seabury Press, 1964); Louis Cognet: *Le Père Teilhard de Chardin et la pensée contemporaine (Paris: Flammarion, 1952); George Crespy: La Pensee theologique de Teilhard de Chardin* (Paris: Editions Universitaires, 1961); Claude Cuenot: *Teilhard de Chardin* (Baltimore: Helicon Press, 1956 [contains a complete bibliography]); Henri de

Lubac: *the Religion of Teilhard de Chardin* (N.Y.: Desclee, 1967); Robert Faricy: *Tielhard de Chardin's Theology of the Christian in the World* (N.Y.: Sheed & Ward, 1967); Robert Francoeur, ed.: *the World of Teilhard* (Baltimore: Helicon, 1961); Christopher Mooney: *Teilhard de Chardin and the Mystery of Christ* (N.Y.: Harper, 1966); Michael Hurray: *The Thought of Teilhard de Chardin* (N.Y.: Seabury Press, 1956); Oliver Rabut: *Teilhard de Chardin: A Critical Study* (N.Y.: Sheed & Ward, 1961); Charles Raven: *Teilhard de Chardin, Scientist and Seer* (N.Y.: Harper, 1962); Pierre Smulders: *The Design of Teilhard de Chardin* (Westminster, MD: Newman, 1967); Claude Tresmontant: *Pierre Teilhard de Chardin* (Baltimore: Helicon Press, 1959); N.M. Wilhiers: *Teilhard de Chardin* (Paris: Edition Universitaires, 1960); Robert Hale: *Christ and the Universe* (Chicago: Franciscan Herald Press, 1972).

19 Teilhard: *The Divine Milieu*, op. cit., p. 138.

Chapter Six: *A New Psychological Age*

1 Cited by Wallace B. Clift: *Jung and Christianity* (N.Y.: Crossroad Publishing Co., 1983), p. ix, Preface.

2 Carl Jung: *Aion*, in: *Collected Works*, IX (II); ed. Sir Herbert Read, et. al., tr. R.F.C. Hull (2nd ed. rev.) Bollingen Series XX (Princeton, NJ: Princeton University Press, 1970).

3 Arthur Diekman: *The Meaning of Everything*, unpublished ms., University of Colorado Medical School, 1770.

4 Cf. Bernard J. Tyrrell, S.J.: *Christotherapy II* (N.Y./Ramsey, NJ: Paulist Press, 1982), pp. 35-39.

5 Cf. Bernard Lonergan, S.J.: *Method in Theology* (N.Y.: Seabury Press, 1972), pp. 6-13.

6 Roberto Assagioli: *Psychosynthesis* (N.Y.: Viking Press, 1971), p. 17.

7 Ann & Barry Ulanov: *Religion and the Unconscious* (Philadelphia: Westminster Press, 1975).

8 Ibid., p. 13.

9 C. Jung: *Collected Works*, IX (1), p. 154.

10 Mircea Eliade: *Myth & Reality*, tr. Willard R. Trask (N.Y./Evanston: Harper Row, 1963), p. 1.

11 C. Jung: *Man and His Symbols* (N.Y.: Dell Publishing Co., 1964), p. 4.

12 Cf. Harry Stack Sullivan: *The Interpersonal Theory of Psychiatry* (N.Y.: W.W. Norton & Co., 1953), pp. 158-171.

13 Dr. Maria Mahoney: *The Meaning in Dreams and Dreaming* (Secaucus, NJ; The Citadel Press, 1976), pp. 26-27.

14 His workshop hs been developed into a book: *At a Journal Workshop. The Basic Text and Guide for Using the Intensive Journal* (N.Y.: Dialogue House Library, 1975), especially pp. 228 ff. Morton Kelsey has written on this same subject from a Christian viewpoint: *God, Dreams and Revelation* (Minneapolis: Augsburg Publishing House,

1974) and: *Dreams: The Dark Speech of the Spirit* (Garden City, N.Y.: Doubleday & Co., 1968).

15 Edward F. Edinger: *Ego and Archetype* (Baltimore, MD: Penguin Books Inc., 1974), p. 146.

16 Ibid., pp. 131-156.

17 Ann Ulanov, op. cit., p. 144.

18 Dag Hammarskjold: *Markings*; tr. Leif Sjoberg & W.H. Auden (London: Faber & Faber, 1964), p. 58.

Chapter Seven: **The Role of Christianity in Building a Better World**

1 A. Hulsbosch: *God's Creation* (N.Y.: Sheed & Ward, 1965), p. 56.

2 Cf.: Irving L. Janis: "Groupthink," in: *Psychology Today* (Nov., 1971); Vol 5, p. 43.

3 Leo XIII: Encyclical: *Rerum Novarum* (May 15, 1891); Pius XI: Encyclical: *Quadragesimo Anno* (May 15, 1931); John XXIII: Encyclical: *Mater et Magistra* (May 15, 1961); *Pacem in Terris* (April 11, 1963).

4 John Paul II: Encyclical: *On Social Concern (Sollicitudo Rei Socialis)* (Dec. 30, 1987).

5 Paul VI: Encyclical: *The Development of Peoples (Populorum Progressio*, March 26, 1967), no. 76.

6 Vincent Cosmao: *Changing the World: An Agenda for the Churches* (Maryknoll, N.Y.: Orbis Books, 1984), p. 57.

7 Synod of Bishops (1971): *Justice in the World*; no. 6.

8 George Mangatt: "Jesus and Service," in: *Jeevardhara*, no. 22 (Alleppey, India, 1972), pp. 276-277.

9 Thomas Merton: *Contemplation in a World of Action* (Garden City, N.Y.: Doubleday, 1971), p. 54.

10 St. Basil: *Homily 12*, 4: *PG* 31, 393.

11 St. Ambrose: *Expositio in Ps.CXVIII*, 8th sermon, 22; *PL* 15; 1503.

Chapter Eight: **The Holy Spirit Broods Over the World**

1 Dr. Larry Dossey: *Space, Time Medicine* (Boulder, CO: Shambhala, 1982), p. 197.

2 St. Athanasius: *Contra Gentes*, 41, p. 26, from the writings of Athanasius in: *A Select Library of Nicene and Post-Nicene Fathers of the Christian Church* Second Series, Vol. 4 (Grand Rapids, MI: Eerdmans, 1957).

3 Emil Brunner: *Man in Revolt* (London: Lutterworth Press, 1939), p. 98.

4 See my patristic study that deals with this subject: *Man: the Divine Icon*, op. cit.

5 St. Irenaeus: *Adverses Haereses*; Bk. V. Ch. 6, 1, in: *The Ante-Nicene Fathers*, Vol. 1, ed. A. Roberts & J. Donaldson (Grand Rapids, MI: Eerdmans, 1957), pp. 531-532.

6 Karlfried Graf Durckheim: *The Way of Transformation* (N.Y.: Unwin, 1988), p. 38.

7 Karl Rahner: *Theological Investigations*; Vol. XVI (N.Y.: Seabury, 1979), p. 204.

8 *The Documents of Vatican II*; ed. Walter Abbott, S.J. (N.Y.: Guild, 1966): *Constitution on the Church*, no. 16.
9 Charles DeCelles: *The Unbound Spirit* (Staten Island, N.Y.: Alba House, 1985), p. 8.
10 P.C. Mozoomdar: *The Spirit of God* (Boston: George Ellis, 1894), pp. 10-12.
11 *The Documents of Vatican II*; op. cit.: *Constitution on the Church in the Modern World*; Preface, no. 2, p. 200.
12 National Conference of Catholic Bishops: *The Challenge of Peace: God's Promise and Our Response* (Washington, D.C.: U.S. Catholic Conference, 1983), p. 36, no. 17.
13 Thomas Merton: *Seeds of Destruction* (N.Y.: Farrar, Straus & Giroux, 1961), p. 234.
14 *Poems by Gerard Manley Hopkins*, ed. N.H. MacKenzie (London: The Folio Society, 1974), p. 62.